Praise for *The Empty Path*

"In a book filled with honesty and heart, Billy Wynne introduces the path of awareness and inquiry through the lens of his own life story, intensely intimate yet at the same time universal and accessible. For each area of focus, a guided meditation supports the healing practice of making real the spiritual life already embedded in our life of today."

— **Karin Ryuku Kempe Roshi, MD,**
co-spiritual director of the Zen Center of Denver

"There are the events of our lives and there is how we experience these events. *The Empty Path* is a heartfelt and wise guide for reflecting on and transforming our most basic assumptions about how we experience time and space, showing us the way toward greater spaciousness and ease."

— **Marc Lesser,** author of
Seven Practices of a Mindful Leader

"Billy Wynne has masterfully written a book that is an expression of the empty path itself and at the same time a guidebook for the journey. By reading words, one can grasp the great reality, and with each chapter in this book, one begins to experience the 'lessening' that Wynne refers to so often. And with this lessening, a lightness of being and innate joy come to life. This book is at once wise and inspiring, tender and loving. It will open your heart."

— **Peggy Metta Sheehan, MD,**
co-spiritual director of the Zen Center of Denver

T0356423

"This is a truly extraordinary and transformative book. It distills the most profound and fundamental truths about happiness and healing to their essence — and it's beautifully written as well. Highly recommended!"

— **Dean Ornish, MD**, clinical professor of medicine at UCSF and #1 *New York Times* bestselling author of *Undo It!* and other books

"*The Empty Path* is a profound commentary on where true peace lies. A counterintuitive approach in a world that is forever caught up in the next thing, this book allows us to calm our minds and open our eyes to the perfection in this moment. I felt both less alone and more alive while reading it. Thank you, Billy."

— **Annie Grace**, bestselling author of *This Naked Mind*

"Billy Wynne gently calls into focus the richness of this moment in his accessible and actionable guidebook for living fully."

— **Sharon Salzberg**, author of *Real Happiness* and *Real Life*

"An engaging, practical, and readable guide to the mystery at the heart of every ordinary moment — the emptiness that Mahayana Buddhism considers the most important thing there is, even though it's not a 'thing' at all. Yet it's the heart of who and what we are, the groundless ground of all our being. Billy Wynne makes tastes of it accessible in this enjoyable offering."

— **Henry Shukman**, author of *Original Love* and cofounder of The Way app

THE
EMPTY
PATH

THE
EMPTY
PATH

FINDING FULFILLMENT
THROUGH THE RADICAL ART
OF LESSENING

BILLY WYNNE

New World Library
Novato, California

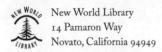

New World Library
14 Pamaron Way
Novato, California 94949

Text design by Tona Pearce Myers

Library of Congress Cataloging-in-Publication Data

Names: Wynne, Billy, author.
Title: The empty path : finding fulfillment through the radical art of lessening / Billy Wynne.
Description: Novato, California : New World Library, [2025] | Includes bibliographical references. | Summary: "Providing an antidote to our culture's never-ending quest for more, mindfulness teacher Billy Wynne shows how embracing the Buddhist concept of emptiness can declutter the mind and distill our experience of daily life to its essential beauty, clarity, and joy"-- Provided by publisher.
Identifiers: LCCN 2024058406 (print) | LCCN 2024058407 (ebook) | ISBN 9781608689613 (paperback) | ISBN 9781608689620 (epub)
Subjects: LCSH: Buddhism--Study and teaching. | Emptiness (Philosophy) | Mindfulness (Psychology)
Classification: LCC BQ4012 .W85 2025 (print) | LCC BQ4012 (ebook) | DDC 294.3071--dc23/eng/20241209
LC record available at https://lccn.loc.gov/2024058406
LC ebook record available at https://lccn.loc.gov/2024058407

First printing, March 2025
ISBN 978-1-60868-961-3
Ebook ISBN 978-1-60868-962-0
Printed in the USA

10   9   8   7   6   5   4   3   2   1

For Harrison and Eleanor

✦

Emperor Wu asked the great teacher, Bodhidharma,
"What is the first principle of the holy teaching?"
Bodhidharma said, "Vast emptiness, nothing holy."
"Who are you, standing before me?" asked the Emperor.
"I don't know," said Bodhidharma.

— THE BLUE CLIFF RECORD

Contents

Introduction

From the depths of perfect wisdom,
the Bodhisattva of Compassion saw the emptiness of
experience and sundered the bonds that create suffering.
— THE HEART SUTRA

If the doors of perception were cleansed,
every thing would appear... as it is, Infinite.
— WILLIAM BLAKE, *The Marriage of Heaven and Hell*

For me, the abundant power and abiding peace of emptiness did not become apparent until the bottom fell out of my life.

I had a relatively comfortable childhood. Crushed oyster shells formed the bed of the driveway leading up to my family's house in rural Chesapeake, Virginia. A hammock rocked gently underneath a weeping willow outside my window. My father was a small business owner and politician. My mother focused on raising my brother and me and taught horse-riding lessons.

When I was eleven, we went, as we often did, to a football game at my dad's alma mater. As we headed home on

State Highway 13, I rested my cheek against the cool window in the back seat of the car, quietly watching the yellow lines stream past in the evening darkness. My father broke the silence by saying, "Boys, there's something I want to talk to you about. Your mother and I have decided to separate." My brother, three years my elder, began to question and protest. I just kept my cheek on the cool window and stared at the yellow lines streaming along the road.

A few years later, on another fall weekend, I was riding with my grandmother. We were on that same highway, but this time we were heading west to visit her son, my dad, in prison. My grandmother kept the car very cool. The frigid leather seats slowed the metabolism of our thoughts. She also comforted herself with menthol cigarettes and Frank Sinatra's greatest hits.

In just those few years, my father had lost his business, his political office, his marriage, and his freedom. The people, places, and paths that I thought supported my life were gone, leaving a void of insecurity and isolation. In response to this formative experience of loss, I embarked on a path of filling my life with *more*.

As an adult, I rushed to accrue the hallmarks of success — more comfort, more wealth, more wisdom, more life hacks — and my fear-driven striving yielded these in abundance. Ultimately, though, they delivered no fulfillment. My adolescent brew of abandonment and anger still seethed beneath my skin, erupting through my calm veneer as outbursts at my wife, my precious children, my colleagues, and my internet technician. Meanwhile, my dependence on alcohol — the deep dive into three martinis on Fridays, the multiple stiff margaritas (i.e., a full glass of tequila with a splash of lime) on Tuesdays (or whenever), my persistent thinking and planning around beverage supply, menus, and hangovers — punctuated my cycles of rage and remorse.

So in my thirty-seventh year I sought counseling for anger management, eventually finding a beloved life coach who taught me the true meaning of responsibility and freedom. I reclaimed my passion for live improvised rock and reinvested in my own musicianship. I picked up Bhante Gunaratana's *Mindfulness in Plain English* and started dabbling in meditation, which led me to the Zen Center of Denver. I stumbled into my first sitting with them and was instantly swept away by the ancient stream.

As my practice deepened and my skepticism of the path of overfilling my life grew, I began to realize that most of the teachings I had explored implied a sense of aspiration, of more work to be done, of wisdom and other spiritual accomplishments to acquire. Even the beloved metta, or loving-kindness, meditations of the Buddhist tradition are couched as aspirational pleas: "May I be *this*." "May my friends and family be *that*."

This train of thought has a sibling: the belief that something is not quite right with us *right now*. That we're imperfect, lacking, in need of a change. It tells us that the truth is located somewhere else, outside us, and that we have to go find it. Every manifestation of our culture reiterates this subtle, pervasive message: There is something wrong with us. Unsurprisingly, we believe it.

Things like material luxuries, esteem, praise, and adoration from our partner become the means of satisfying the self we see as somehow incomplete. Even our quest for spiritual growth and lasting peace can become another way of finding contentment via accumulation. Signing up for the next wellness regimen can give us a stronger dopamine hit than the program itself. Whatever it is, we believe that the next thing *out there* will be what finally settles our anxiety and fulfills our dissatisfaction.

It wasn't until my forty-fifth year, careening down the highway on the way home from the alcohol-free bar I had created to cultivate peace and community, with one knee on the wheel and my thumbs on my phone, prepared to accept a horrific crash as a preferable alternative to this unbearable stress, that I finally realized the path of more-ing has a dead end. It was suddenly obvious that it was all a lie.

With the debris swept away, all that was left was a simple truth: *There is absolutely nothing wrong with us. We are fundamentally perfect, complete, and whole. Lacking not a single thing, we are free to be at peace in this moment and come forth in harmony with all that is. We have always been so and always will be.*

Whatever our circumstances, no matter how dire, we can experience true, abiding peace. There is nothing else we need to do, nowhere else we need to go, nothing outside us that we need to aspire to, work toward, or learn. Every single thing about us and all beings is just as it ever could or should be. Everything we could ever need is right here, right now.

The reason this is so — the solitary, ever-present realization that can unlock a life of peace, freedom, and fulfillment — is emptiness.

Recognizing this opened my eyes to the fundamental beauty and preciousness of each moment and inspired me to begin practicing the radical art of lessening. I closed the bar, refocused on my connections with my dearest others, and re-committed time to embodying peace via meditation. In this simple clarity, I've been able to repair my relationships, find ease in my work, enjoy play, and relish the quiet comfort of each breath. Yes, challenges still arise — frustrations, arguments, mistakes, loss — but my relationship to the cycles of life has fundamentally changed from resistance and denial to gratitude and often awe. This is the path I want to share with you.

The Irony of Emptiness

It may surprise you to hear that emptiness is the portal to ultimate fulfillment. Most self-help books, including many inspired by Buddhism, tend to skirt past this core teaching as they evangelize the path of *more*. Western culture trains us to think that emptiness is synonymous with worthlessness, meaninglessness, or apathy. You may be concerned that pursuing the path of emptiness will cause you to isolate yourself from loved ones, and reject your deepest values or overlook the suffering of others, the injustice of systems in which we live, or the harm we cause.

But, in fact, realizing the emptiness of things can empower us to overcome the numerous filters and obstacles we put between ourselves and these precious and important aspects of our lives. By allowing us to see through the surface of our ceaseless judgments, the path of emptiness weakens our cravings and aversions that skew our perceptions and prompt our reactive, counterproductive behaviors. What is left is the simple beauty of our experience and our underlying unity with all things. When we can set aside the ultimately arbitrary labels we put on our experience — once our "doors of perception" are cleansed — we see our inherent, unbounded wholeness. We see that nothing in fact separates us from that thing we crave or the person we loathe. Arriving at each new moment this way, we are free to navigate life with joy, ease, and compassion, even in the face of sadness and loss.

The irony of emptiness is that it exists side by side, moment to moment, with our experience of everyday life. They are not separate. This laptop in front of me and this book in front of you are real; their atoms are indeed swirling just so; their colors and textures are arriving at our eyes and fingertips as we perceive them to be. Realizing emptiness does not mean that your coffee cup is going to fall through the table and shatter on the floor.

At the same time, all these things are empty. The way we experience, judge, and identify them is temporary and arbitrary. No one facet of them makes them what they are — there's no coherent, abiding source of identity, the "self" that we ascribe to them. Seeing through their illusory facade, even as we type on or read them, is the gateway to our liberation from fear, anxiety, and regret.

After exhausting every other strategy, from excessively indulgent hedonism to total ascetic abandonment, the Buddha saw the emptiness of all things, of every manner in which we experience our lives, as the Heart Sutra says. It was this profound insight that enabled him to "sunder the bonds" — abandon the attachments — that create suffering. By taking up this practice, exploring the truth of emptiness, and applying it to our own lives, we can do the same.

Back to Earth

I wish I could tell you that embracing emptiness has completely eliminated all my attachments and suffering, mistakes
and frustration, but you are probably well aware that's not
how life works. There is no mountaintop where, once we
reach it, we can just recline and watch our concerns disappear. Life isn't a hill, it's a wheel, and the wheel is always
turning. Every day, I engage with the practices I will share
with you. Every day, I experience the arising of attachment,
fear, anxiety, and regret. Every day, I intend to acknowledge
these aspects of my experience, recognize their emptiness,
and then let them pass through.

Nonetheless, I know that today I will say something that
is less than ideal to someone I love. The question is, how will I
work with that experience? Will I cling to my judgments and
dwell on my imperfection, spiraling into self-loathing? We
all know where that path leads. Or will I acknowledge what
I did and pause for a moment to take a good honest look at
what happened? I can call to mind my inherent wholeness
and the wholeness of the person I love, and I can see the
fleeting and also precious nature of the moment we shared.
Then I can move a bit more peacefully into the next moment.
Maybe I need to apologize or offer some other repair. Either
way, there's a new word, a new action, a new moment coming.
Will I enter into it encumbered or free? Here I am not refer-
ring to a freedom that ignores our circumstances or pretends
they are otherwise. It is a freedom *within* our circumstances,
just as they are, to embrace and cherish the precious moments of our lives. This is the daily practice. These are the
stones along the empty path.

REFLECTION: How Was Your Day?

Take a moment to consider what's true for you today. What did you do earlier, and what was your experience of it? Perhaps your morning was filled with peace and joy; I certainly hope it was. Perhaps some challenges arose: a difficult encounter, an unfortunate word, a worry, a regret. That would be quite normal. You would not be alone with that one.

Now just pause and revisit whatever that moment was. Bring it back to life here with you. Being here now doesn't mean we erase our memory; we can choose to be present with an experience to reconsider what it has to teach us. In fact, as we will explore, simply "letting go" of the past isn't the healthiest way to find our peace with it. It's only with an authentic turning toward our experience that we can truly reconcile with it and take our best next step.

What do you see in that moment? What do you hear? Who is that person you were, doing whatever it is you were doing? How does it feel to reembody it? Has anything changed for you as you look at that memory anew?

As I will often recommend, try to resist the urge to rush into these questions with answers. Hold the questions aloft. See if you can just be with the inquiry for this moment. Let it linger and illuminate the experience you had, and try to avoid applying snap judgments or labels. It might help to bring attention to your breath — not to change or manipulate the breath, just to recognize that it's happening. Let it fill you up and ease your mind. Your practice has begun. The empty path is under your feet.

Taking a Seat in Emptiness

To begin our inquiry into emptiness, let's explore getting a whiff of it for yourself. This may feel a bit wonky or confusing and that's okay. I invite you to breeze through it with levity. Perhaps set down your immediate instinct to agree, disagree, or fully understand. Let the words do the work.

Are you sitting on a chair right now, or can you see one nearby? We don't tend to give a lot of thought to calling this thing a chair, resting on it, and going about our business with it underneath us. But what makes it a chair? Is it the legs? If we just had the legs, would we call that a chair? Do the legs give it its "chairness"? I don't think so.

What about the seat? If the seat were lying there on the floor, would we call that a chair? No, the seat doesn't make a chair a chair. It must be the backrest, this part we're leaning on. No, without the other pieces attached to it, I'm not sure what it would be. So it must be all these things together. When you consider all the components as one, you have a chair, right? Well, if I remove the seat so you just have a frame with legs and a backrest, we'd probably say that's a chair that's missing its seat. So it's not actually all the things together that make this a chair.

A whole lot more goes into a chair being a chair, anyway: the metals that were extracted from the earth; cotton and other materials that were harvested and woven into the cushion of the seat; miners and farmers and factory workers who fed their efforts into the construction of the thing; the designer, the manager of the production process, those people's mentors, and all facets of their life trajectories. All these things led to the existence of this chair. They are a part of what makes it what it is. Yet not one of them is a chair in and of itself.

With so many different things contributing to the chair, and not one of them being something you can point to as a chair itself, maybe all that's really a chair is the concept of this thing that lives in your mind. The label is useful so you don't have to consider the infinite sources of its being all the time, but perhaps we can acknowledge that we're using a label, a figment of thought, to establish this idea of a chair, which, on its own, is also not a chair. So the idea of a chair isn't a chair, and the chair isn't a chair. Voilà: There's no such thing as a chair. It's empty.

And so is everything else — you, me, and every aspect of our lives: our past and future, the space we inhabit, our thoughts, our relationships. Our minds tell us a story about these things that assigns them a coherent identity and permanence they don't actually have. In that instant, we step out of inherent, undifferentiated wholeness and into an unquenchable separateness. Having instinctively constructed our idea of that thing, we know from then on that it can't be us. Once it's on the outside, we are compelled to assess its benefit or detriment to this thing on the inside that we call our self. In other words, we judge.

This intuitive response can be obvious ("I don't like grapefruit") or subtle ("This pen will work fine"). Often our judgment of the object of our attention may be mixed ("This couch is comfortable, but I don't like the color"). It may be easiest to think of these two categories of response as those aspects of things we find "acceptable" and those we find "unacceptable." We have a strong instinct to see things this way, born of our need to quickly assess potential threats during the eons we spent as vulnerable hunter-gatherers. But this predisposition to define everything as beneficial or threatening, which extends beyond mundane objects to include major life events, other people, and our deepest values, solidifies an avatar of that thing in our minds, which obscures its (and our) essential truth.

Reacting to our experience this way — perpetually oscillating between attraction and aversion, craving and fear — is the essence of suffering. Realizing the emptiness of all things, then, is the vehicle for abandoning our attachments and living a life of liberation and joy.

Science gives us another lens for understanding emptiness. The components of our reality — the swirling atoms and their various parts, the firing neurons and their perception and reinterpretation in our minds — are all lacking an inherent identity. They're empty too. If the nucleus of an atom were the size of a golf ball, its closest electron would be about a mile away. If the mass-bearing elements of all the atoms in a skyscraper were smushed together, removing all the empty space between them, you'd be left with something about the size of a Tylenol capsule. Take another look at that house or building next door. What do you see?

Furthermore, the location of those electrons and other particles is essentially impossible to pinpoint. The elementary components of atoms can exist in different places at the same time — it's only when someone observes them that they finally "pick" a place to be. This stuff around us that we perceive as hard-and-fast, fixed and lasting, is primarily empty space, occupying an uncertain location, perpetually arising and receding. No matter how hard we try, we can never find anything to actually attach to.

What can we make, then, of these innumerable forms and experiences that arise and fall and collide and rebound in an unimaginable symphony of being? Perhaps the best we can call it, borrowing the words of Tibetan teacher Yongey Mingyur Rinpoche, is infinite possibility. It's the unimaginable origin of all that has ever been and will be — always becoming, always re-creating, always new.

Let's pause to bring this closer to home. Over the course of your day, what might it be like to call on this awareness? Each encounter, each blade of grass we step on, has arisen from an infinite, undefinable array of origins. Here it is for us now, and it will continue to unfold into an equally infinite and undefinable future of its own. What a miracle that it's here! Moreover, because we share its emptiness, we are not separate from it. There's no need to pursue or avoid it because it is already us.

This awareness allows us to enjoy the beautiful bare simplicity of our life just as it is. We can stop being preoccupied with accumulation, with more-ness. We can turn toward the difficulties in our relationships and the injustice of our world, and we can apply a peaceful heart and gentle hand to their healing. Our work can be inspired, our play creative, and our love unfettered.

With this elegant nature of being always present, this open invitation to the release of our suffering, *why do we seem to miss it at every turn, even outright resist it? Why do we stand in the way of true joy? Why do we deny ourselves our birthright?*

Why Letting Go Doesn't Really Help Us Let Go

Perhaps we have at times recognized that the path of more-ness — suffering in our work, accumulating material luxuries, and signing up for self-help programs — may not give us the satisfaction we seek. But instead of allowing this awakening to bring us into balance with our lives, we tend to bungee over to the polar opposite: a newfound faith in "letting go."

It is enticing to believe that we can simply abandon our problems, drop our offenses and grievances in the wastebasket, and just go about our business. I used to pretend that I'd moved past my family's disintegration, for example, which provided some temporary relief from the pain I felt. But I was just flipping the coin of attachment to craving on its other side — from attachment to aversion — and my suffering inevitably returned.

If we simply view these aspects of our life as harmful and neglect giving them due attention, we miss the opportunity to truly examine what they mean. Uncovering their deepest truth is a vital step along the path of emptiness. Maybe you had an unpleasant conversation with a loved one recently. You could just "let it go," and that may briefly mute the anger or regret you feel. But if you do that, you will never really see yourself and that person clearly in that moment. You'll never hear the words that were spoken fully. You'll never explore the feelings that arose for you. If you let all that go, you don't resolve it, you just bury it below a thin veneer of abandonment or accommodation. We tell ourselves we're free from it, but it's still got an invisible hand on our wheel, subtly guiding our behaviors.

We can only understand the truth of our experience by

embracing it, reconciling with it, and turning toward it. Take another look at yourself in that moment, at that person you had the conversation with, and at the words that were spoken. If you listen to, and let yourself feel, all the aspects of what transpired, *what might you find?* You'll never find out if you just let it go.

In a recent conference call for a board on which I sit, another participant's comments deeply troubled me. I found myself in fight-or-flight mode, questioning my participation on the board and the other person's motives. The road before me diverged into several paths, with one offering the choice of combat: I could go on offense, attack that person's motives, and aggressively defend my position. Another path offered retreat: I could just "let it go," shut down, and avoid any further contribution to the topic. Perhaps I'd just resign from the board altogether.

A third path offered something very different: to stand still, right there in the moment, to fully acknowledge what was happening, and to take a step inward to its truth. First, I noticed the tension in my body, the tightness of my stomach, the escalation of my tone of voice. Second, taking a breath, I revisited my core intentions for arriving at that moment with the board: I truly cared about its mission. Third, I recognized that, however we might disagree, everyone else taking the time to contribute to this discussion was essentially coming from a place of positive intention. I reminded myself that how we board members were engaging each other now would strongly influence the outcome we were collectively seeking.

Then, as I looked even deeper, the distinctions between

me and the other participants, the flurry of concepts and labels I had assigned to each of us, began to dissolve. Yes, here we are, bringing unique life experiences and points of view to the discussion. And, at the same time, each of us shares the same absence of essential selfhood; we are united in our emptiness. From this place of heightened awareness, I can be at ease, and my best next step can be honest, respectful, and compassionate. I can honor my experience and point of view — and theirs — but the emotional charge is gone, tempered by recognition of our mutual participation in the beautiful simplicity of being. That's a far cry from the bitter warrior who would have charged into battle with them if I hadn't taken this brief pause.

Understanding and living by the emptiness of things starts with allowing ourselves to settle enough that we can see them clearly. We focus on them, ease into them, and empower ourselves to recognize the emptiness they share with us. All things, like us, have arisen temporarily and without any specific feature that gives them a distinct, independent identity, as we will unpack, in much more detail, throughout this book. This realization creates a fundamental change in our relationship with our experiences. We don't (and can't) abandon these experiences because they are not separate from us. Indivisible from them, we are unified in the inherent wholeness and sufficiency that includes all things. Then we are free to be with any experience with our deepest integrity, in the love that allows for its infinite possibilities to unfold.

The weekend before I wrote this, my son came home with news of a disappointing setback at school. Despite his best efforts, he'd found himself in significant trouble. Tears streamed down his face as he expressed his shame and anxiety about his mistake. The particulars of this situation matter: what he did, the teacher's response, his taking responsibility, and the consequences to come. It is important to honor the validity of my and his emotional responses to these realities. We share regret for the incident, confusion about what to do next, and fear about the repercussions on his schooling and broader social development.

At the same time, I can recognize that at the crux of my immediate reaction is my ever-threatened ego self, the one that produces and receives — and is in fact defined by — these types of judgments. If I just accept all the components of this situation as separate, including the teacher, my son, and my thoughts and emotions about it, I will miss out on the abiding source of unity, comfort, and peace that is also always present. Each aspect of this situation is empty, arising from the same origin of indivisible, consummate perfection. This is where grace resides: in the space between my conditioned reaction and a centered, inspired response. My twelve-year-old son may not intellectually grasp this yet but, as I embrace this mindset as we deal with his situation, he can sense the change in my demeanor — my posture, tone of voice, and gentle eye contact — and tune in to harmony with my lead.

Approaching the encounter with my son this way, I see that there is nothing for anger, shame, or fear to attach to. There is only the plain matter before us and the next step to take. I know that my ability to convey this peace to him will not be as artful as it could be; I know that whatever comes next in this chapter of his life will include additional pain and discomfort, and that sadness weighs on my heart. But I also know, and deeply trust, that buoying myself with conscious remembering of my own emptiness and the emptiness of all things empowers me to be the best possible father I can be at that moment: a little less regretful about the past action, a little less attached to the outcome, a little more peaceful and clearheaded in lending a hand to my son.

There is nothing special or magical about this. The empty path just requires putting one foot in front of the other. I hope this book provides a lamp for your journey.

The Art of Lessening

To take the empty path is to occupy this middle ground between more-ing and just letting go. It's the art of lessening — of distilling, essentializing, focusing, and letting the natural radiance of things shine forth. This book will provide you with tools, detailed practices, and inspiration to follow this way through the reality of your daily life.

This is a transformative path. The art of lessening, an embrace of emptiness, offers a gentle reorientation of your life. As you investigate it, reflect on it, and practice it, you might begin to notice subtle changes in your relationship to your experiences. Here are a few examples.

Instead of striving for more-ness, you begin to settle into enoughness. You feel simple, abiding gratitude for the staggeringly improbable miracle of your being here at all. A single instant, a single breath, is a lavish gift. Instead of harboring anxiety or longing about what has passed or is to come, you develop an openhearted honoring of what is, a balanced place from which you can offer life your best response.

In lieu of searching, you realize what's already here. As I sit here in this coffee shop, searching for the right words, the pile of lemons in the bowl in front of me gleams crisp yellow, gently dimpled skin, and a collage of shadows. Everything is present. Nothing is missing.

Rather than pretending to know, you give in to your childish curiosity. Moving beyond any compulsion to make things happen, you can allow your participation in creation to unfold. Attachment to outcomes in work and play then gives way to equanimity, the space where openhearted improvisation — also known as fun — can flourish.

You release mutual dependence on others in favor of the truer love that honors you and them as you are, uniquely doing what you each do. You don't have to expend tremendous effort to make connections. Rather, you recognize connection as fundamentally true. Kindness is no longer an ethical obligation but the natural response to the truth of coexistence.

Your mistakes and painful regrets find rebirth as forgiveness and responsibility. In emptiness, there is no place for blame or shame, because there's nothing for it to attach to. There's only your participation in the cocreation of each moment, without bounds. We are uniquely free and solely responsible.

Notions of self and other, scarcity and attachment, give way to wholeness and inherent fulfillment. Nothing was ever missing from you; you just imagined it so. The dissatisfaction that sat uncomfortably in the sidecar of your daily experience is fundamentally resolved. Everything is vivid now, calling to you, reminding you of the beautiful totality of all that you are. With fresh eyes, you see the flower, the fork, the friend.

With genuine wonder, you are present for the abundance of life rushing in.

The tools with which you will hone the art of lessening are made up of mindfulness, the essence of the practices I will offer you for deepening your personal experience of the teachings offered in this book. Mindfulness as presented here began as Vipassana (or Insight) Buddhism, which has flourished in Southeast Asia for millennia. Meanwhile, the Zen I describe initially took shape in China, was further cultivated in Japan, and then traveled to the United States. Both streams emerged here in earnest in the second half of the twentieth century. I began studying Buddhism and mindfulness practices thirty years ago and received certification to teach in the Insight tradition from Jack Kornfield and Tara Brach. I entered the stream of Zen ten years ago and received lay ordination (called *jukai*) in 2020. Now I serve on the board of the Zen Center of Denver and teach classes in mindfulness and Buddhism there. My intention with this book is to combine these profound teachings with the very practical ups and downs of my own life to offer you a straightforward, relatable path that doesn't require any background or belief in Buddhism. At the same time, it is important to acknowledge that, while the practices as I present them have become Americanized in some ways, they are not American. I offer homage and deep bows of gratitude to those Asian masters who, in their compassion, have shared with us these profound teachings.

Your Empty Path: How to Use This Book

The Empty Path is a how-to manual for the art of lessening — for realizing and practicing emptiness in the vivid texture of your daily life. With a bow to your life circumstances and lived experience, I would like to walk side by side with you on a hero's journey: from our miraculous birth where we come to understand our being in time and space (the first three chapters) to hearty engagement with life in relationship to those around us (the next four chapters) and onward to transcendence, which is more akin to complete immersion than a departure (the final three). Each chapter will invite you into the emptiness of a facet of your life and offer you ancient wisdom, modern examples, and clear practices for cultivating your understanding of it.

Sprinkled throughout each chapter are reflections meant to deepen and illuminate your experience of this practice. And at the end of each chapter are practices in the form of guided meditations. Reading them through once or twice will help you get started. You can practice them slowly, mindfully, for about ten to fifteen minutes each time. Or you can spend more time with them, depending on what your schedule allows. Audio recordings are available to assist you with your practice at BillyWynne.com.

The path of emptiness is illuminated by ancient Buddhist teachings that we'll explore, applying them to the present reality of our daily lives. We'll get deeply acquainted with one such teaching in each of the ten chapters. I'm not asking you to "believe" them; I offer them as tools for fostering your own understanding. I invite you to investigate them with an open heart and discover their meaning for yourself.

It may be most helpful to read the book from beginning to end, but you might also find you'd like to skip to a chapter that calls to you, perhaps an aspect of your life that is giving you difficulty at that moment, before moving on to another that invites your attention. Your natural curiosity, your knowing intuition, however and whenever it arises, will empower your understanding of *The Empty Path*.

I invite you to give each element of the book a try, and I hope and trust that some will serve you. You may adopt some and disregard the rest, a natural practice of lessening. This is not an invitation to accumulate another prescribed doctrine. Nothing presented here is any more sacred than the paper it's printed on. Finding your balance with it will unveil the exquisite truth of you. I am not a master or guru of any stripe who has attained something that you have not. I hope that this book is valuable to you for the precise reason that I am walking alongside you on this journey, sometimes skipping on a hillside, other times wading through the mud.

At the same time, I acknowledge that you bring your unique life experience to this voyage, most likely including a considerable degree of hardship and pain and, too often, injustice and oppression. Sadly, our culture of more-ness feeds on and fuels disparity in all its manifestations. Perfectionism and endless accumulation are the parents of systemic oppression. *The Empty Path* is not about denying or bypassing this reality; it is, in fact, about facing it directly and responding appropriately. It does not neglect the basic human rights to dignity, safety, and material security that we all deserve. We will explore this more along the way, particularly in chapter 6, but please do not misunderstand any teaching here as denying the validity of your life experience or the motivation you may have to advance justice.

Also, if a teaching or practice presented here arouses any

trauma you may hold, I encourage you to modify, pause, or simply abandon what's offered when necessary to recenter yourself. Such episodes of self-care are not deviations from the practice; they *are* the practice. The fundamentally peaceful presence that is you abides all the while.

This is the nature of emptiness. It is subtly but indelibly interwoven with the substance of our daily lives. It is not the slightest bit separate from the tree outside the window, the chair beneath you, or that ID wedged into your wallet. If we just see the bark, or the fabric, or the plastic, we've missed the real story it has to tell. The story doesn't change anything about it, but it tells us the difference between attached suffering and liberated joy. Looking closely and calmly, the pages unfold by themselves, and the timeless truth is revealed in an instant.

Suffering and dissatisfaction, longing and fear have had their turn. Right now is the moment of your freedom. Right here is the arising of your joy. Right in the midst of it all is your reunion with everlasting peace.

MEDITATION: Emptying Your First Step on the Path

So here we are, my fellow traveler, about to begin our journey together. I'm grateful for this opportunity to embark on it with you. I offer you this brief guided meditation practice as a means of orienting your compass as you approach the path ahead.

Take a moment to settle into your space. Perhaps you are sitting, letting yourself be held up by your chair. Let your feet rest on the floor, feeling its gentle support. Try to trust for a moment that everything you could possibly need is already right here.

Notice the fact that you are breathing. Without the slightest effort, feel the cool breeze coming in and out of your nose, feel the rhythmic rise and fall of your belly. Let a gentle smile curl your lips; your breath will be your fuel for the journey ahead. It will always be right here with you. Let your attention rest on your sensation of the breath for just a few moments.

Now consider this book you are holding in your hands, this combination of paper and ink, of harvesting and refining, writing and editing, printing and shipping. The empty path you are about to travel rests in its pages. Where did it come from? Where were the trees that yielded this paper, the machines that applied the ink, the vehicles that carried it to you? What point in this long process of creation makes this book what it is? As it sits here in front of you, what fragment of this object gives it its bookness? The spine or the cover? One of the pages or all of them? Is there anything here — has there ever been anything — that we can say makes this book a book?

There's no need to generate answers right now. See if you can just lean into the questions and find some spaciousness in these mysteries.

Broaden this awareness to your expectations for reading the book. What ideas and preconceptions have you brought with you? What perceived problems are you trying to solve? What gaps do you hope it might fill, curiosities it might quench? Take a moment here and give each idea or problem that comes to mind a deep bow. They have served to bring you to this moment, but they are not this moment, and they are not this book. Let their energy fill you up completely and then gently pass through.

Take a deep breath. Here you are. There's no book in front of you. No expectations behind you. No path ahead of you. There's only this precious moment we get to share together and this undefinable inspiration we have to take one step forward. We cannot know where it will lead. As we pause for a moment to appreciate that space, to immerse ourselves in not knowing, here it is. This new moment has arrived.

Chapter 1

Reclaiming Time

At this very moment, what is there outside us,
what is there we lack?
— ZEN MASTER HAKUIN'S *Song of Zazen*

Breathe. Breathe in the air. Don't be afraid to care.
— PINK FLOYD, "Breathe (In the Air)"

For several decades, I was five minutes late to just about everything. I resisted time. I refused to accept its subtle truth, the story it wants to tell. I can't say exactly where it came from, this vague unease. Like everything else we avoid, though, it followed me, producing a considerable amount of anxiety and regret.

I developed this unsteady relationship with time in my teens. My comfortable upbringing trained me in the traditional path of believing proper execution of preceding moments — with their efforts and intentions, plans and expectations — yielded predictable benefits in the future. If I would comply with my parents' and teachers' instructions and otherwise lay a sturdy foundation for my life to come, I believed, then comfort and fulfillment would naturally unfold.

Early on, my father's life appeared to embody this theme. Having embraced his intellect in high school, he graduated from the University of North Carolina, served honorably in the military, and achieved success in business and local politics. His and my mother's marriage also mirrored this traditional ascent: high school sweethearts who built a happy life with two kids in the brick-hearth den and dogs playing in the newly seeded yard.

As I entered early adolescence, though, I began to notice subtle changes in our household. My parents began to have extended closed-door chats on Saturday afternoons. My father was more frequently absent, physically and mentally, from our home. Soon enough, we were in that car ride heading home from a football game and, as he announced their separation, the predictability of time's march unraveled for me.

Here is the story of my parents' divorce. One Sunday afternoon shortly after their separation, my mother took my brother and me to my dad's house for a visit. We were right on time. As we approached his small bungalow, the faded blue Honda Civic of the woman for whom he'd left my mom, whom I had not yet met, sat outside.

My mother walked, guardedly, up to the front door and rapped on the thin vinyl facade. Several moments passed with no response. She pushed aside the thorny bushes in front of the nearby window and peered inside. Again, she knocked on the door. More moments passed. Eventually, the door creaked open and my father was standing there, his clothes wrinkled and untucked, beads of guilty sweat appearing on his face. My mother marched in.

In deference to everyone involved, I won't detail the ensuing moments. Suffice it to say that we walked back out of the house a few minutes later. My mother took me and my brother to Hardee's for soft-baked cookies. We ate silently while enough time passed for my stepmother-to-be to leave my dad's house so that we could return. It was only a few years later that my father's second marriage was over too, along with his business and his tenure as mayor, as he sat in the proceedings that would lead to his imprisonment during my junior year of high school.

Due to the public nature of his position, all these developments — the divorce and its aftermath, his political turmoil, his conviction and prison sentence — played out on the front page of our local papers and the opening segment of our local newscasts. As my friends, teachers, coaches, and the checkout person at the grocery store looked on, the life I knew disintegrated. The moral of my adolescent story was that everything we know and trust to be true, that we depend on for peace and security, is an instant away from destruction, and there's nothing anyone can do or say to stop it.

I had associated myself with the traditional idea of linear, ascending time and invested all my earnest planning and expectations into obtaining the fruits of the future. Now that path had reached a dead end.

Arriving Now

Thich Nhat Hanh, social activist, prolific author, kind teacher, and greatly realized Zen master, said, you "have an appointment with your life.... [It is] the present moment. If you miss the present moment, you miss your appointment with life."

Wherever you've gone, whatever you do, all you have ever been is right now. Yes, a chain of events has unfolded in your life. You have a history. But where is that past? Can you show it to me?

Consider if perhaps what we call our past is just a cohort of ideas. It consists of memories — some cherished, some regretted — that exist only in our mind. Try as you might, you cannot call forth any element of your past. You cannot manifest it. It's not *here*, and you certainly are not *there*. You may often reside in it, in a way. Many of our thoughts relate to the past. We can become so consumed by them that it can feel as if we *are* there. Memories, faulty as they often are, can be so intense that they spawn physiological responses. In those instances, however, all we have conjured is a projected image, a movie on the screen of our mind.

That's not to say it's wrong to have memories. Learning from our experiences can be incredibly valuable, serving to wake us up to what's present. At the very least, perhaps we can agree that the past is not real for us *now* and we can never truly *be* back then.

What about the future? Consider whether any facet of the future is here now and whether it could ever be. Yes, of course thoughts about the future arise — hopes and dreams, fears and worries. Our emotional responses to these thoughts about the future are also real. We'll get to that later. But when the event occurs that we had dedicated time to expecting, what is it then? It's the present. Here we are — now — experiencing that thing we invited or dreaded. Often we discover that what actually occurs is far afield from the expectations we held. Our experience of it is an entirely different matter from our thoughts about it, just like reading the menu and looking at the photos of a restaurant online bear no resemblance to sitting in the cushioned booth with friends and eating a bowl of pasta covered in spicy sauce.

No matter what your mind tries to tell you, the truth is that you have no choice but to be here now. You were never and can never be in the past. You are never and will never be in the future. You are now. With this keen eye, you can see through your yesterdays and tomorrows to arrive only at what is present. Here's the beautiful thing: That presence is always here. It never goes away, whether or not we're looking at it. The door to the here and now is always open, inviting us in.

The Emptiness of Now

Let's pause to consider, then, this present moment. This place where we exist. Tell me, what sliver of time is it? How long does the clock tick when it's "now"? If we look very closely, we might see that the present moment is just a dimensionless boundary between the past and future, neither of which are here. Hm.

Science tells us that what we call time is in fact amorphous, fluid, and flexible. It changes with movement and is inextricably intertwined with the three dimensions of space. We prefer the idea, perhaps cling to it, that time is fixed and unchanging, with clearly defined boundaries and increments, the clearest of which is the present moment. Like other ideas we will explore, we believe this helps us organize our life experience. In each stride of the march of time — past, present, future — we believe we have found something to hold on to.

The tighter we squeeze, however, the more elusive the

true nature of time becomes. We may believe we have found an answer to life's riddle — focusing on now — that will give us abiding peace and fulfillment. We look again, though, and poof; it's gone. Try again to show me the present moment. Where does it begin, and where does it end? What is happening in this moment? Too late. It's gone.

In this way, we may see that even the present moment is empty. It does not have clearly defined boundaries — no inherent, consistent identity. Given all we've been taught throughout our lives, this slippery aspect of time may feel a bit unsettling at first, but it can be the gate through which we enter into the true and everlasting peace we deserve.

Consider that when we understand time as fluid, with the present moment being an invisible boundary between past and future, there really is no distinction between a millennium and an instant. Each is infinitesimally small, a brief syllable amid the infinite expanse of time. Each is also infinite, containing innumerable, infinitely divisible syllabic multitudes. As William Blake said in his poem "Auguries of Innocence," you can "hold infinity in the palm of your hand and eternity in an hour." Time is unbounded and free and thus so are we within it. As our attachment to time as fixed and unbending begins to fade, we discover our freedom. What arises in time's place is the beautiful fertile soil of a comforting truth that will never fail us. Past, present, and future are all equally here, equally accessible to our timeless being.

Thus we unpeel the first layer of the onion we are exploring together. Each of these aspects of life has its own wisdom to share, and each has just one thing in common: emptiness.

It's only with this understanding that we can truly embrace Thich Nhat Hanh's admonition. What was he pointing to when he called us to the "present moment," that standing appointment we have with our life? Somewhere in our marrow, we already understand. Let's keep exploring to rediscover it.

Choosing Our Experience of Time

Consider the last time you were at an airport (or train station or bus stop). For me, for so long, my experience with these places was all about time. Starting the day before, I'm thinking: I need to wake up at x time because it takes y minutes to get ready for z's drive to the airport and zz's check-in and so on and so on. How long will it take to get through security (that great equalizer and eraser of time)? Will my flight be delayed? Times are posted on the arrival/departure boards. Times are lit up on the gates. I'm hustling, a bundle of bags and anxiety, restraining myself (at best) from snapping at my children if they pause to ask a question while I futz with the kiosk to print a luggage tag. This experience is deeply unpleasant, and it's all about *time*.

What's the alternative? Am I suggesting that you sleep through your alarm, lallygag on your way to the airport, and miss your flight? That you just ignore time altogether? Not at all. As we will see with each of the aspects of our lives that we'll explore in this book, acknowledging time's emptiness and experiencing its deepest truth is a far cry from pretending it doesn't exist.

In fact, it's the opposite. The alarm still rings and we still get ready. We still consider the time needed to drive to the airport and we still might wonder whether or not we'll be on time. The difference lies in how we choose to experience each of these moments. It's whether we confine ourselves to the dominion of time or immerse ourselves in it to unveil the illusion of its boundaries. Seeing through the illusion of past, present, and future, how might we greet the alarm? How might we step to the closet? How is our heart as the amoeba of our family (or just ourselves with our bags and thoughts) traverses the airport terminal? Isn't it interesting how time shrinks when we're rushing to the gate and then expands when we sit and wait for the boarding call? We aren't turning away from any of these steps. We are turning toward them, perhaps grateful for the next opportunity to experience what is arising, whatever it may be.

On the conveyor belt carrying us through the terminal to our gate, it can be a joy to breathe in this explosion of life. Here we are with so many people in their comings and go-ings, their dreams and regrets, their abundance and loss. Each person, each moment, offers an ineffable story. In my better moments, I let a grin come to my face. The clocks around us all are ticking, and yet here we are in this unimaginable moment. The miracle of being has arisen, and we get this precious opportunity to take note. If I didn't want to catch my flight, I might just fall on my knees and bow.

REFLECTION: Painting the Next Moment

What's another way to access this experience of time? Let's pause for a moment. You are invited to pull out pen and paper and write down these thoughts as they arise. As ever, there's no need to create a Hemingwayesque masterpiece. Just let the words fall through you and onto the page.

Turn your mind's eye to your past, maybe just the collage of images that arise when you revisit what you did yesterday. You woke up, and then what? You probably ate a few times. You may have gone somewhere, or maybe you just traveled around your home. You may have had some conversations. Just take a moment and look at those many images, one by one, as they appear in the kaleidoscope of your mind. Write them down. They are as real as the chair you sit in and this book you hold.

Staring at those still frames in your mind, let them start to fade and blur, as things do when we hold our gaze on them longer than usual. Examine them like a watercolor painting that has not yet settled on an edgeless canvas. It has space to include all these many memories. Viewing the thought images side by side, let the colors bleed and swirl. They may be bright and bold or soft and blurred. Maybe you are having trouble recalling what you did yesterday; it happens to me all the time. The images are just shades of gray. That's perfect.

Now grab your mind brush! This is your palette. You choose where to dip the bristles. You have a new canvas in your life today, waiting for the artistry of your love and creativity to paint. Take a moment to breathe in, acknowledge, and relish your freedom. There is a wide array of tints for you to choose from. They are yours and yours alone. No one else's hand is on the brush, and there are no edges to the canvas. Where is the past now, and what defines this moment? Take your first stroke. What images appear?

Nica Time

During the winter term of my sophomore year of college, I had the privilege of living with a family in León, Nicaragua, as part of a sister city service program. Every weekday morning, I would catch a *communeta* bus to a nursery, where I volunteered to assist with hybridizing different plant species. The entire experience was life altering and a story of its own for another time. The smell of woodstove smoke always reminds me of walking through the dusty streets of the town and of the warm smiles on the faces that greeted me there.

One of the many lessons I learned in Nicaragua was the concept of "Nica time," the locals' understanding of time and how they practiced it in their daily lives. In brief, it means that hours and minutes have soft edges. If you agree to meet with friends or work associates at 2:00 p.m., the last person might not arrive until 2:20, or sometimes much later.

The underlying rationale for this approach, among the many you might imagine, is that there is always space to engage with people you may encounter along your way to such a meeting. There is never a need to say, "Sorry, can't talk now. I've got to be somewhere at two." In my entire time there, I never once observed what Benjamin Hoff identified in *The Tao of Pooh* as a "bisy backson," a reference to the note the ever-anxious Rabbit would leave on his front door in Pooh Corner. "Busy. Back soon."

In this way, the local Nicaraguans were generous with themselves. They were never short on time, always having as much as they felt they needed. Time there was abundant and graceful, not the domineering drill sergeant we so often consider it to be in the US. They were certainly aware of time; they didn't deny the trajectory of the sun overhead throughout the day. Not at all. But time was a facet of life at their disposal, to engage with on their own terms, in a way that supported their deeper priorities and values.

I am not prescribing Nica time to you or our culture as the remedy for our anxiety or a hack to meet the demands of our lives. I am not saying to start arriving everywhere twenty minutes "late." I share this story to demonstrate that time is much more malleable than we tend to believe and to encourage us to loosen our attachment to it. How we conceive of time and integrate it into the practice of our lives is, in fact, up to us, individually and collectively. Time is a mindset, no more and no less. Instead of serving it, we get to decide how it can serve us.

The Impermanence of Time

The Buddhist teaching of impermanence offers additional insight into the emptiness of time and can support our liberation from its presumed constraints. Taught by the Buddha and cataloged in some of the very earliest sacred texts of the tradition, impermanence is considered a fundamental aspect of all things — *every single thing*, including the tree outside, you, me, and time.

Impermanence speaks in part to the fact that all things live and die. For nonliving things, like stones or chairs, we might instead say that they come into being and eventually cease to be. This is an aspect of life with which we are already very familiar but perhaps prefer to ignore. Something very powerful within us wants to hold on, to keep that thing or person we cherish here with us for as long as possible, sometimes forever.

Yet we know this is not possible. The tree outside our window wasn't always there. At some point, a seed transformed into this tall, lush green being that shades our lawn and fuels our breath. And someday it will pass away. Whether it is chopped down or simply dies and decays, at some point in the relatively near future it will go away, it will no longer be a tree.

This too is the case with the monuments we build, the treasures we keep, the people we love, and the moments we share. Somewhere, at some time, they arose out of the innumerable conditions that were necessary for their being: the materials, the events, the convergence of nutrients or other building blocks, the efforts, the love. Then each of these conditions eventually disentangles from one another and that object or life is no more.

As you can see, impermanence is not a minor detail of our lives. The sign over the old Zen Center of Denver temple quoted Zen master Dogen: "Great is the matter of life and death." The Japanese American Zen master Shunryu Suzuki said, "Life is like getting on a small boat that is about to sail out to sea and sink." Our awareness of our own mortality, and that of those we love, is perhaps the fundamental riddle of life and the source of our deepest pain and suffering. Resolving that riddle may be a key reason you picked up this book. It is a key reason I am writing it.

How do we resolve it? The first step is to resist our likely predisposition to turn away, to consider this subject too heavy for us to contemplate and skip along the surface of our lives in willful ignorance of this ever-present, underlying truth. Rather, we can turn toward it with an earnest intention to investigate this principle of impermanence and what it can teach us about ourselves and our lives.

In doing so, we may begin to understand another illuminating aspect of impermanence. Yes, things arise, live out their existence for a certain time, and then pass away. Also, everything is always changing. Different from what it just was, each thing arises anew in each moment. We might say that it is reborn.

Take, for example, that tree outside your window. It was probably born many years ago and probably won't die for many years hence. Just as important, though, is the fact that it is different now from how it was yesterday or even moments ago. It has grown; some leaves have sprouted and others have fallen; its bark has gradually faded; its sappy innards have oozed. The tree that it was when you started reading today is no longer there. A new tree was born the instant after, and again and again until right now, and so it will always be becoming a new tree, never quite the same tree again. That's the heart of impermanence, and it is true for you and me and all things. Just look and see for yourself.

Applying this point to time as we experience it in our own lives, we might begin to understand that impermanence is not really about how things end. Each ticking moment is not a march toward death and decay, forever lost to a nostalgic past. Each moment is a renewal. It is a rebirth. By embracing the fact that time, like all things, is always changing, we take an essential step toward lessening our attachments and rediscovering our lives. Then time is the source of our liberation from suffering and freedom from the dominion of death.

REFLECTION: Linger with Gratitude

This feels like the right spot to give you a moment to pause and reflect on what has been presented so far. Again, I encourage you to pull out a pen and paper if that suits you. Perhaps start by considering a person, place, or thing in your life that you cherish. If it's easier right now, it can be something as simple as this book in your hands or the cup on the table beside you.

Take a moment to let yourself be grateful for something you value. It is wonderful that it is so. Nothing here is intended to deny that. Savor your feelings about it for a moment. Then consider, where did it come from? From where did it arise? What elements and preconditions were necessary for it to come into being? How long will it last? Where will it go when it's gone?

Now look again. In what way is it changing right now? If it's alive, this may be more obvious. If it's not, without diving too deep into chemistry or physics, perhaps consider how the materials that make up that thing — the atoms and elements — are constantly swirling, reorganizing, combining, colliding, fusing, and dividing. Consider how your appreciation of that thing, your use of it, its location, has changed and will probably change again. Also, all the while, it is slowly, invisibly decaying, as all things do.

How does your relationship to this person, place, or thing feel now? I'm reminded of teacher and writer Tara Brach's words regarding each aspect of our life: "It's passing and it's precious." Maybe you can begin to glimpse how this truth of impermanence, this ostensibly sorrowful aspect of life, can be the portal to a profound connection to everything around us, a deeper love for what is.

The Art of Lessening Time

With time being perhaps the quintessential thing that we never seem to have enough of, in our days or in our lives, it may seem contradictory that the path of liberation from its constraints is paved with lessening. But this lessening is not about wasting time or frivolously giving it away. It's about relaxing our grip on time or, rather, its grip on us, to lighten its weight, free ourselves from the regret and anxiety it often brings, and traverse it with buoyancy, clarity, and joy.

The linchpin of this method, as we will see again and again, is to turn toward the object of lessening — in this case, time — completely and wholeheartedly, to immerse ourselves in awareness of it so that its truth can unfold before us. This is the essence of mindfulness that we will apply to the various aspects of our lives examined in this book. It is the practice of paying attention to what is present without judgment.

A key practice to consider here is simply noticing. Your attention can be broad: to the whole field of your experience of time — the hours and deadlines, the regrets and anxieties, the cherished memories and dreams — or it can be narrow: to the ticking passage of it as you experience it right now. We will apply the essence of these techniques to other aspects of our lives, but the common thread is simple awareness, with nothing added. The beauty and irony of this practice is that, when we distill our attention, everything tends to become more vibrantly alive; we allow its inherent abundance to shine through.

As we notice, it is equally important to cultivate a bit of gentleness, openness, or kindness. Whatever we're experiencing, positive or negative, our intention can be to simply see it for what it is, staying in that place that exists before the natural instinct to judge arises. In his poem "A Great Wagon" Rumi wrote,

Out beyond ideas of wrongdoing and rightdoing
there is a field. I'll meet you there.
When the soul lies down in that grass,
the world is too full to talk about.

Lessening creates spaciousness. We don't have to accept whatever is here, but we can make room to acknowledge it.

What does this mean in the context of your day-to-day life? Look at your watch or the time on your phone. Look at the clock on the wall, the planner on your desk, the calendar on your computer. Regard the sun as it inches across the sky. Note the moonrise and the shifting constellations of stars. There are so many emblems and indicia of time in your life. Each one is in fact precious; as with all things, it is calling to you with the same persistent message: right now is your opportunity to awaken to your life, to be present with each moment.

Pause to consider the typical thoughts and feelings that arise for you when you glance at these things. More often, at least with regard to watches and calendars, they may provoke stress, anxiety, concern, hurry, or distraction. Maybe the more natural manifestations of time (the sun, the moon) are a gentler place to start. Whatever you choose to consider, preferably something that is nearby right now, take a moment to regard its details — its color, shape, location. Now to let in a deep, nourishing breath. That's all. Just breathe and keep looking. Let your gaze soften. Let your thoughts settle. Is anything changing?

Maybe so or maybe not, but you have begun to retrain yourself. "Checking the time" can be an opportunity for you to practice a brief moment of mindfulness. It's not something to avoid; it's something to relish. You get to decide to make it so and, with a bit of practice perhaps, it will be.

Reflecting on Resistance

Even though we are just getting started, it would be unusual if you hadn't already experienced some degree of resistance or self-doubt about engaging with this practice. Have you noticed that yet? Have you, like me, had thoughts like "I'm not cut out for this," "I'm too busy for these pauses," or "My mind's too scattered; that's just who I am"? And so on. I think any of us who has encountered these practices has had some version of these thoughts. Go ahead and take a moment to write down your version of them right now.

This is why, with mindfulness and all the other practices I will share with you, the most essential step is to put aside whatever expectations you may be carrying for what it *should* be like or what you should be like when you are doing it. This can be particularly challenging when almost everywhere we look — social media, the magazine stand at the grocery store, billboards — we see images of "Zen-like" states of bliss, almost always eerily cast in the same sunset, experienced by people who don't look like anyone I've ever seen, apparently generating states of mind that I, for one, have never felt.

These images and motifs might lead you to believe that you can only experience "true" mindfulness in a Tibetan monastery or some other remote place, far from the hustle and bustle and stress of your daily life. Please just forget about all that. This is one of the many ways we're told that we are not enough, that we need to be more in order to find true peace. Please don't believe those lies.

It's actually right here, in the context of your life — yes, right now — where you can mindfully awaken. It's at the traffic light, on the Zoom conference call, in the argument with your spouse. That's it! Right there. This is, after all, what your life is. The door to mindful, compassionate presence is always open to you, and the *practice* of realizing it never ends. "The Buddha is still sitting," we say in the Zen tradition. There is no end goal, no permanent state of disembodied ecstasy (sorry) to be attained. We are simply manifesting an intention to return our focus to what's here again and again (and again…).

So be loving and patient with yourself. Even for those who have been practicing for many years — decades — we are all, alas, still human. I don't know of any gurus who levitate above the ground or float through every instant with ease and consistent precision. As far as I can tell, every human being continues to encounter frustration, disappointment, and sadness. Nothing presented in these pages is going to eliminate unpleasant experiences, the arising of negative thoughts and emotions, or mistakes. What this practice can do is help us change our relationship with these experiences. As Jon Kabat-Zinn said in *Wherever You Go, There You Are*, "You can't stop the waves, but you can learn to surf."

You are here, right now, with an intention to take a step forward. That intention is enlightenment itself. One of the progenitors of American Zen, Yasutani Roshi, liked to say that 5 percent sincerity is enough to start with. Please keep that footnote in your pocket. Just sit down. Just breathe. That's all it is. It's all you need to do. Perhaps you will even enjoy it.

More good news: like a muscle, mindfulness can grow

with exercise. It will deepen in time, become a bit easier to settle into, even become routine. And mindfulness doesn't go away, just like the truth of the present moment of your life never goes away. It is always available to you, however shrouded by your life circumstance it may seem. It's always right here, right in front of you, inviting you to be aware, to relax, and to come forth in love.

The Moment of Breath

There may be no simpler or more readily accessible method for reorienting our relationship with time than focusing on the breath. For starters, it is always with us, always present. It is simple and automatic; it doesn't require any planning or maintenance. Your body knows how to breathe. Because it doesn't require any conscious action, breathing can show us how to let things be. As we deepen our focus on it, our relationship to what's before, what's now, and what's to come begins to shift.

Breath is also an indication, your many life circumstances notwithstanding, that everything is essentially okay. As Kabat-Zinn also said, in *Full Catastrophe Living*, "As long as you are breathing, there is more right with you than there is wrong." If you're breathing, then you are here and you are where you belong. Breath can remind us that our sacred home can be found wherever we are.

At the same time, breath is indisputably impermanent. It arises and falls, comes and goes. In that way, it's an incredible teacher, an ever-present reminder of our deepest truth. It sits at the intersection of all that we are, manifesting in the world, and reminds us that it is always changing. So how do we cultivate mindfulness of it?

The Buddha taught four essential postures for meditation: sitting, standing, walking, and lying down. I recommend starting with sitting, and you can explore the other postures later. Sitting can be done on a meditation cushion or simply in a chair. I won't go into the details of the various cross-legged positions one might take on a cushion. I invite you to explore those on your own if you are interested.

Wherever you sit, and regardless of what posture you take, there are just a few key principles to apply. The first is stability. You want to find a position where your body can be still and at rest. In a chair, this means finding one at a height that allows your legs to rest comfortably and feet to land flat on the floor. It means letting your arms and hands rest comfortably in your lap.

For your hands, you might also choose to explore the mudras (hand gestures) and other positions various traditions advise. For now, what matters is finding a resting place that is comfortable. For me, this means putting my dominant hand (my right) flat in my lap and letting my nondominant hand (my left) rest flat on top of that. Thanks to my Zen training, I cup my hands slightly and let the tips of my thumbs touch gently. That's my mudra. You can find your own.

Try to keep your back straight and your head up. This promotes optimal blood and energy flow throughout the body and helps maintain alertness. It also allows you to relax the rest of your body while maintaining your posture. I like to think of my spine as a coatrack and the rest of my body as a raincoat, hanging effortlessly from it. You can let your shoulders drop as you gently lift your head further and elongate your spine. Another nice trick is to imagine there's a small hook on the crown of your head attached to a string that is kindly tugging it upward. Sit like a mountain, with dignity, honoring the loving intentions that brought you here.

And the last guideline: perhaps do it with some levity and gratitude. We aren't digging for oil here. Let a soft smile curl your lips. Sometimes the grin on our mouth follows the arising of happiness within. Other times, the expression on our face comes first and the internal feeling follows. Sometimes we spark, other times we're sparked. Meanwhile, we're cultivating our appreciation for the privilege of sitting here in a moment of peace.

Okay. You have found your seat. Now we begin.

MEDITATION: Breathing Time

Finding a posture that is gentle and alert, let's begin with a few deep, cleansing breaths.

Give yourself permission to relax, settling into a spirit of stillness and balance.

Notice any areas of lingering tension in your body. Offer those spaces some gentle breath; see if you can relax them a bit more.

Let your head lift gently; let your spine lengthen. Whether they are closed or dimly open, let your eyes be soft.

Now notice the fact that you are breathing.

Take a moment to locate the part of your body where your experience of the breath is most prominent. It might be your upper lip, the tip of your nose, or the back of your throat, or it might be the rise and fall of your chest or belly.

Wherever you are drawn, that's the right spot. Just let your attention rest there. Be with your breath.

With curiosity, notice the texture of your sensation of the breath. It may feel short or long, warm or cool. Notice the space between breaths — where they end and where they begin again.

Consider practicing kindness in your attention. There's no need to judge or try to change the way you are breathing. The breath is doing what it does. Just notice.

You might try some skillful ways to maintain your attention on the breath. Perhaps let your mind's voice name the inbreath as it ebbs and the outbreath as it flows. "Innnnnnn." "Ouuuuuuuut." Let the sensation of the breath and your silent naming of what's happening fill you up completely.

You might also try to count the breath, perhaps on the exhale. After breathing in, let the thought of "Onnnnne" fill your heart-mind as the breath flows out of your body. Allow the count to resonate inside you from the very beginning of the outbreath to the very end. With the next exhale, "Twoooo," and so on, until you may arrive at ten, when you can start the count anew.

Quite soon, usually before you get to ten, your mind will wander. It's no problem. That's what the mind does. Just as the glands secrete enzymes, the mind secretes thoughts. There's nothing wrong with that. There are times to plan and wonder, solve and dream. We're just not going to water those flowers right now.

As a thought arises, just let it float by, like a cloud in the empty sky, like a bubble of water floating to the surface. Give it a kind nod and then return your focus to the breath, starting again at one. Recognizing that your mind has wandered is a perfect instant of mindfulness. The "goal" is not to count to ten. The goal is to pay attention to this one breath right now.

This is the heart of the ancient practice. Returning, again and again, to the breath, to mindful awareness. When our mind wanders, we notice and return. Notice and return. That's all it is. The last breath is gone. The next breath will come on its own. There is just this breath. And now this one — moving gently through, unstuck and effortless.

Continue now, breathing and noticing. Wandering and returning. Settle into your practice. You are at your timeless home.

In the final moments, perhaps consider a bit of gratitude for the breath. It has traveled a long way to get here. What a miracle it is, always arising, always falling. Let's not miss it.

✦

How did that go, my friend? How do you feel?

Perhaps for the first time, you are confronting your "monkey mind" face-to-face. It can be alarming to realize just how frantic the mind is, almost maniacally leaping from idea to idea, plan to plan, regret to regret, fantasy to fantasy.

There is nothing wrong with you or how you are doing this. For beginning (and deeply experienced) meditators, there's no greater obstacle than self-doubt. We'll come back to this voice in your head, our frenemy who loves to tell us how unworthy we are. Please just give it a kind bow and tell it "not right now."

Perhaps you are surprised by the simplicity of the practice. Maybe you arrived expecting to learn magical spells or esoteric rituals that will instantly absolve you of your problems.

Fortunately for both of us, I don't have anything complicated like that to offer.

The simplicity of the practice — returning again and again to focus on the sensation of the breath — is its essential characteristic. This is how we soften the regrets and anxieties of our time-driven life. There is no equation to solve or complex process to follow. The recommendation, here and ever, is to let such notions pass and allow the simple clarity of the moment to arise. What if that's actually true of every aspect of our lives? What if we gradually unwind our complexities and our underlying faith that they will give us peace? What if our life, with all its twists and turns, is not actually a problem to be solved? What then?

This simple practice is exactly how we strengthen our mindfulness muscle and cultivate our capacity for loving presence that is free from the self-imposed boundaries of time. This is how we realize the life-affirming power of emptiness.

Chapter 2

Belonging in Space

He looked around him as if seeing the world for the first time.
The world was beautiful, strange, and mysterious. Here was blue,
here was yellow, here was green, sky and river, woods and
mountains. All beautiful, all mysterious and enchanting.
— HERMANN HESSE, *Siddhartha*

The earth where we stand is the pure lotus land — and this very
body, the body of Buddha.
— HAKUIN'S *Song of Zazen*

After my parents' divorce, I would periodically stay with my father and stepmother in the small bungalow they had moved into. For me the walls and furniture of that space contained the trauma of my parents' fissure and all the discord that ensued.

My father did his best to help me feel at home. My bedroom was appointed with baseball memorabilia and a framed puzzle that we put together after visiting the Hall of Fame in Cooperstown years earlier. Overall, however, with the exception of our beloved sheepdog, Daisy, who stayed with my dad, the space reeked of unfamiliarity. The smell of the burgers he fried for us for the first time, the whiff of thin paisley upholstery on the newly purchased couches, and the emblems of his marriage to my stepmother filled me with the uncertainty and instability of the unknown.

I spent many of my hours in that space playing Nintendo, particularly Tetris. The bright geometrical balance of the pieces falling down the screen offered some temporary relief from my discomfort. At night I would lie in bed and see images of those pieces raining down in my mind's eye, sustaining their useful distraction until I faded off to sleep.

Also at that time, I doubled down on my investment of time, energy, and money in my baseball card collection. I had begun it years earlier when the fragments of my life were more coherent, and it was my prized material possession. Being above average in both an affinity for rationality and social awkwardness, I treasured the time I spent alone, putting the elements of my burgeoning collection in good order, dividing them carefully by year, assigning them by brand and numerical position in their respective sets. I alphabetized the star cards and admired the trim evenness of their protective plastic sleeves lined up neatly in four-rowed cardboard boxes designed for this purpose. Most of all, I enjoyed the act of accruing. The sight of several full boxes of cards, regardless of their content or value, stacked up in the corner of my room, was a shrine to *more*, a ballast of perceived abundance that supported me during this tumultuous time.

The space most impacted by this time in my life was my body. This was when I learned how to be numb. Unable to fully understand, much less emotionally process, the disintegration of my family and other hallmarks of stability in my life, I dissociated from my bodily experience of them. I have no recollection of how I actually felt at that time. All I remember is dullness, like I was floating through tepid water, ignorant of the sensations attendant to the ascent or decline in feeling that each new life event brought. Here too I adopted the pathos of more-ness to blanket my pain. I developed a preoccupation with diet and weight lifting as remedies for my muddled body image and distractions from my chaotic feelings.

During high school, while my father was in prison, two caring teachers asked me to join them in their office after I'd acted out disruptively in class. They said they had noticed some changes in my behavior and asked if there was anything weighing on me that may perhaps be prompting this trend. I considered their question for a moment, thanked them for their concern, and answered truthfully that I had no idea what they were talking about. I had completely disassociated from the obvious facts of my unfolding life.

At about the same time, and by now we were in our third home in just about as many years, my father and stepmother sat me down for a discussion. They expressed their concern that I was treating their house like a hotel rather than a home. I came and went with minimal interaction with them and my stepsisters, focused instead on heading back out as soon as possible to a friend's house, a party, the gym, or a walk alone on the beach — somewhere else.

I share these vignettes as illustrations of living in dissonance with the space we inhabit — with our surroundings, our possessions, and our bodies. The amalgam of my experiences during this phase taught me that I do not belong where

I am and that my body is severable from my self. Of course there is nothing wrong with a child collecting baseball cards, playing Tetris, or struggling to connect with a new stepfamily amid tumultuous circumstances. But I believed, as perhaps we all often do, that objects outside me, material possessions or locations I occupied, were either threatening bearers of pain or abiding sources of comfort. All the while, I suffered. Only later did I realize that, for the entire time, I was right at home, always belonging, never actually disconnected from my body, my environment, or my possessions.

I just sold my baseball card collection and have set the money aside to spend on some experiences with my son, who's now an avid sports fan. No longer dependent on the collection for comfort, I love all that it has meant to me more than ever, even though it now belongs to someone else.

Realizing Our Home

As with time, we are trained to believe that the material world — the space we inhabit, the stuff we have, the places we go, the body we're in — is not quite right for us. It is never "enough"; we are contemplating either imperfections that must be improved or pleasures we hope will persist. These judgments cloud our perceptions and render us attached to things as positive or negative. Too often we traverse our lives like a pinball bouncing toward the illuminated bumpers and their validating chimes and off the agitated flippers that we believe will protect us from the depths below. Never quite occupying our true space, we proceed in a state of persistent reactivity.

There is of course another path, and it is already beneath our feet. On this path, we see through the distracting blinks and bells to the underlying truth of every place we are and everything and everyone we encounter. Each is tenderly impermanent, always arising anew, and each lacks any inherent identity that separates it from us. When we understand it this way, we see there is nothing to crave or fear, because nothing is set apart. Everything is exactly where it belongs, a unique gleaming facet of the ever-brilliant jewel that we and all things are.

To live this way is to always feel at home. Wherever we are, we belong. Whatever we have, we understand will pass through. Whatever we don't possess, we know is not separate. Yes, of course we each need and deserve food on our table, a roof overhead, and clothes to keep us warm. Some of us may have those things in abundance; for others obtaining them is a daily concern. Wherever we fall on this spectrum, what can change is our relationship to these things and to ourselves as well. We can freely arrive and depart, give and receive. The pinball machine falls apart and there we are, at peace.

The Emptiness of Space

Space is time's companion in the framework of our reality, the stuff that comprises our material world. As with time, we afford things a permanency and an identity that give them considerable power over our lives — whether it be via attachment to a home, a vehicle, or other asset as a facet of our personality or a location that we glorify as a portal to peace and well-being (the hillside retreat, cloistered monastery, or pristine beach). This attachment can also arise in the form of aversion to a childhood home, that lemon car, or features of our body.

As with the nature of the chair we explored in the introduction, every facet of space is empty. We can apply the same method for recognizing emptiness to any object, like any of the baseball cards in my collection, a few of which I kept for my son. As I look at one now, I see cardboard and pigment, names, letters, and numbers. It is strikingly unique and complex. Which aspect of it makes it a baseball card? The cardboard that it's printed on? The ink that combines to present an image of a player, their team logo, and the brand of the card? The historical data and statistics enumerated on the back? Or how about the moment that snapshot of the player, swinging at a fastball, was taken? Perhaps it's the production process in which thousands of these cards were printed on large sheets, precisely cut, reshuffled, and packaged into cellophane wrappers. Back in my day, they were combined with gum that would occasionally leave a rectangular stain looming over the information on the back of the bottom card.

Of course, not one of these things makes the baseball card a baseball card, and not one of them, if removed (as sometimes happens with production errors), would make this card something else. Nothing we can point to makes it what it is, other than the ideas and labels we attribute to it in our minds. Put more fancily, the card has no inherent identity, no "self-nature." It is also indisputably impermanent, since it was manufactured a certain number of years ago and sometime soon will disintegrate back to dust. At the same time, incalculable causes and effects with no identifiable origin in time or place have given rise to this precisely shaped, brilliantly glossed, elegantly light object that is indeed sitting carefully in my hand right now. What is it?

Let's widen our lens now to consider our sense of place, the space we occupy. Right now you may be sitting in a chair in a room in your house, or maybe you are on an airplane, on a beach, or in your bed. What makes the place we occupy the place we believe it to be? I'm reminded of a quote from the great Lieutenant Frank Drebin in the movie *The Naked Gun*. After taking a long walk, staring at his feet as he reviewed various aspects of his case, he looks up and tries to recall: "Where the hell was I?"

If we pause to consider it, every aspect of our location is relative, in flux, impermanent, and empty. We sit somewhere among the cardinal directions relative to our earth as it spins on its axis and orbits the sun. Our solar system is circum-ambulating our Milky Way galaxy, which is on a journey of its own. Bear with me if this isn't as fun for you as it is for me, but perhaps consider: The earth spins at 1,000 miles an hour; it rotates around the sun at 67,100 miles an hour; the sun and our solar system orbit the Milky Way at 514,000 miles an hour; and the Milky Way is hurtling through the universe at about 670,000 miles an hour, depending on your reference point. Where are we, exactly?

You might find an exercise like this interesting, boring, invigorating, or a bit unnerving. The intention is to support you in relaxing your grip on what it means to be "here." Again, we have been trained to believe that we can clearly identify where we are on a map, amid structures and objects that we can define. In one way, albeit a relative, ever-changing way, this is true. We depend on these reference points to navigate our lives. At the same time, in an equally true way, our understanding of these reference points is just a product of our mind's inclination to label and categorize. Their reality and our perception of them are always changing, even if subtly, in every instant, and lacking a singular, fixed location. What they are is no more real than what we happen to decide they are. These two ostensibly contradictory features of our reality peacefully coexist, undivided reflections of the same underlying truth.

REFLECTION: Take Note of Where You Are

Where does this leave us, then? We might be intrigued at the thought that the space we occupy may not be exactly what we thought, but soon we are going to stand up from our chair and head to the kitchen to make lunch, or put this book down on our bedside table, rest our head on a pillow, and fall asleep. So what difference does this new perspective make?

This would be a good moment to pull out your pen and paper or simply pause for some quiet reflection. Take in your surroundings. Regard the structures and objects that constitute the place you are in. Go slowly. Name them. Let your attention linger on each aspect as you notice it arising in your mind. Observe its characteristics — its colors, its location, and any glares or shadows cast. Turn your eye inward and examine the thoughts and feelings each object elicits for you. Is your experience of it pleasant or unpleasant? Does it carry emotional weight for you, or is it relatively unimportant, your relationship with it light?

Go on like this for a little while, perhaps five or ten minutes. Really examine and immerse yourself in your place. Take inventory of the abundance around you. Wherever you are, I bet there is no end to the possible places to lay your attention, large and small, near and far. Consider that there is color and texture and distance at play. There are items you are touching and those you aren't. Also consider how each of these things is changing right now and will change over time. Consider that their various characteristics, including their location, are relative to those of other items nearby. Consider that nothing around you possesses any particular aspect that truly makes it what you think it is, other than the thought label you have given it in your mind. Just rest with this notion for a moment.

Now tell me: What is near and what is far? What is same and what is different? Where do you end and these things begin? Is that boundary of your skin really so definite? Now tell me: What's pleasant and unpleasant? What resonates heavily and what doesn't? You are still in the same place among the same things, but maybe something has started to change. When you take the next step to leave the room or go to sleep, what exactly are you leaving behind? Whatever new posture or space you are moving to, how is your relationship to it different from what it was in the place you were just before? Perhaps each new place you go, this is exactly where you are. Maybe no matter where you stand, you are actually right at home.

The Interbeing of All Things

You may have explored and had some personal experience with oneness. Something organic in the human experience, if we can settle ourselves and relax our minds, allows for the notion to arise that all things share some common identity. But what does this really mean, and what can it teach us about our experience in the world?

On one level, we can observe the interconnection among things, what classical Buddhism calls (somewhat inelegantly) "interdependent co-arising." No person is an island unto herself, and nothing appears out of thin air. Everything is contingent on the causes and effects that precede it, creating a symbiotic web where all things support each other's existence.

Starting from the beginning, we and all things on the earth somehow derived from the basic elements of stardust that coalesced to form our planet over 4 billion years ago. Right now all things are constantly shedding the cells and atoms that make them what they are, cells and atoms that go on to make other things. On a larger scale, trees nearby exhale the oxygen we breathe in; the soil to which we all return nourishes the food we eat; a gust of wind on the dry plains of the Serengeti shifts the moisture-rich clouds over the Rocky Mountains outside my window.

On an interpersonal and cultural level, we can see just how interdependent we all are. The choices we make in our workday and careers, at the dinner table and through the course of our family relationships, at the voting booth and in our engagement with our communities throughout our lives — all these actions impact everyone around us directly and all beings around the world indirectly. Likewise, our lives have been influenced and shaped by the actions of our parents, our teachers, our friends, and the social and cultural norms of our time. We are contributors to the causes of these things and recipients of their effects.

The way in which each of us and all things fuel the cycle of creation is an important aspect of the Buddhist principle of interdependent co-arising. Here, as elsewhere, however, the tradition recognizes that this perspective addresses only one side of our reality: the relative side, the side that reflects the typical way we experience our encounters with the world around us. This is the world of form, where all things are differentiated by their characteristics of size, shape, color, and other expression.

Another side of our reality, equally true and always present, is not separate from the relative side but perfectly interwoven with it. This is what Buddhists call the absolute aspect of things, the way in which nothing has a unique, fixed identity unto itself, in which their underlying emptiness is apparent. From the absolute perspective, all things are not just interconnected; they are undifferentiated, each being an infinitesimally temporary manifestation of the whole of all existence. They don't just interdepend, they *inter-are*.

This is how the emptiness of the material world — everything that surrounds us — serves as the gateway to our liberation and peace. Impermanent and lacking any notion of a core identity or definable boundaries, no one object can be distinguished from another or this place from that. There is no separation. This is what William Blake points to when he beckons us "to see a world in a grain of sand and a heaven in a wild flower."

Revisiting a Journey

An interesting way to bring this teaching, which may feel a bit heady or esoteric, back to the context of our lives is to recall a vacation or other trip you took in the past. Our experience of a new place can give us a unique perspective on how we experience our space in the world.

Before you left home, you probably had some well-formed ideas about how you would feel once you reached your destination, what your trip would be like, and the types of experiences you would have there. You may have visualized the terrain and surroundings, the lodging, the views. You likely had expectations of how this experience would be different from your typical day at home.

Then you went. You traveled and you arrived and then you were there, waking up in a bed, taking a step. What was that experience actually like? Try your best to summon the textures and smells, the events and interactions. Maybe you can visualize yourself, the same you sitting here now, navigating it all. Maybe your experience of the place was unique to its characteristics, the features of the landscape, the weather, the people and their habits. Maybe some of these experiences have a pleasant resonance for you and others less so. This was your experience of the relative aspect of that place, in which you were interconnected with the people and places and things you encountered.

At the same time, thinking back, you might notice the person who traveled to that place was a different person from who you are sitting here right now. That experience shaped you and changed your course to the present, whether incrementally or drastically, not to mention all that has happened since. Also, reconsider those things you encountered from the perspective we applied to the chair or baseball card collection. They had unique features, yes, but did any one of those features make it what it was? What part of the wave you surfed made it a wave? Which aspect of the cactus that pricked your leg during a hike made it a cactus? Which shade of auburn, feathery wisp of cloud, or sublime ray of light made that a sunset? Wasn't each of these things just a snapshot along its path of perpetual flux, each new moment revealing a new iteration of itself, its impermanence on plain display? How did that aspect of experience differ from where you were before you left? Were you really any less at home on that trip than you are right now?

The intention here is not to judge vacations — large or small, near or far — as good or bad. It is to help us realize that, wherever we are, we have an opportunity to awaken to the precious truth of our lives, which is not contingent on the ever-changing nature of the place we inhabit. As Thoreau wrote in his journal, "It matters not where or how far you travel...but how much alive you are."

Lessening Space through Embodiment

There is no more intimate way to distill our experience of space in the world to its essential truth than through awareness of our body. While I certainly hope all the words offered to you so far in this chapter support your realization of the nature of space, our body already "knows" what it is and where it belongs. Often our thoughts and ruminations just get in the way of our direct, embodied experience of our lives.

Our body, on the other hand, has no choice but to be with the true nature of what is, effortlessly unifying the relative and absolute aspects of our being right *here*. There's no space in our body for thoughts to get in the way. Our bodies, whatever we may think of them, can be among our greatest teachers and pathways to true awakening and freedom.

If you're like me, it's easy to get so cerebral that we believe our thought life is our real life and we turn away from the reality of our embodied experience as we try to solve the puzzles of our lives. Maybe, like me, you've believed you can simply think your way past a problem and move on. Many times I've told myself I'm over a traumatic event from my childhood, for example, only for that experience to manifest in my shoulders or my gut. The mind may forget, we say, but the body remembers.

Perhaps fortunately, then, we are stuck with our body and what it reminds us of. We find that ignoring what it tells us usually just makes things worse. There's a common misperception about mindfulness and meditation that I've brought up before — that we're seeking some sort of blissful state apart and away from our physical incarnation, some disembodied experience. Actually, it's the opposite. The way to resolve our suffering is to turn toward and embody what's here.

So where do we start? If we pay attention, we may find that all our thoughts and emotions are usually accompanied by physical sensations. They don't arise in a vacuum. To take one everyday example: If we're nervous about what we're doing, we probably feel that familiar tingling or churning in our stomach. If we're feeling anxious or angry, perhaps we feel tension in our jaw or shoulders.

To embody the experiences of our lives, then, to observe and participate in them most fully, we can be mindful of the sensations that arise with them. This provides a root for our experience that we can trust as authentic. Our simple but not easy embodiment practice is just this: We try to pay attention to the physical sensations in our body, whatever they may be. This is not always easy because it can be uncomfortable to focus on unpleasant sensations. We're not used to it. We've been conditioned to contract from or avoid discomfort. We may also find that we've been trained to pursue pleasant feelings and try to make them last. The more we judge or try to control our sensations, though, whether it's pushing away or hanging on, we're injecting our mind into the matter, filtering our experience with judgments.

So a key element of the practice is to let the bodily experiences be what they are. Notice them, acknowledge them, honor their truth, and then let them go on their way. They will not last. What's it like to just notice that our feet are cold or that our back has some soreness, or that our arm has some tingling? What's it like to just observe and not identify with or attach to these perceptions?

A helpful tool for accessing the body can be to simply ask yourself, "What's happening in my body right now?" This is the noticing aspect of mindfulness. Taking the practice deeper, we might ask, "Can I be with this right now? Is there space for this here?" This is the kindly act of nonjudgment.

Another powerful tool for inviting attention to the body is to feel from the inside out. Try this quick experiment that I learned during my meditation teacher training, in a talk given by Tara Brach: Rub your hands together for ten to twenty seconds. Pay attention to how they feel, brushing against each other, swishing by. Notice any feelings of rough or soft, cool or warm. Then stop and hold your hands apart in the air. What do you feel now? Perhaps you notice there is still much aliveness present, some tingling or vibration. This is feeling from the inside out.

In these ways, through our bodies, we can practice

abandoning the deeply ingrained instinct to crave or suppress our sensations. By watching them arise and fall, we experience their emptiness, which in turn strengthens our muscle for connection and presence. Even when we feel pain, we can try to simply experience it. I find it is a helpful practice to name the sensation: pressure, cramping, throbbing. To further acknowledge and practice being with this experience of our body, we can verbalize allowing it with a soft "yes" or "this too." Here again we are applying mindfulness to transform discomfort or pain into a doorway to awakening.

This is not about powering through pain, though. As with all practices presented in this book, this one is not a substitute for medical care when that may be necessary. Likewise, if the pain you're focused on becomes so strong that it's harmful to your presence and well-being, the invitation is to simply redirect your attention to another sensation of the body or, if the pain is extreme, to take a break from the practice. Certain sources of pain and discomfort may even be associated with past trauma and can quickly become overwhelming.

As always, discernment and self-care are paramount; take a pause if the practice isn't serving you, and use additional tools or get help if you need it. We can expand our capacity to be with what's here and, at the same time, engage with the practice of our inner knowing of what's best for us. We will explore the principle of ahimsa — nonharming — later on, but this guidepost applies to us as well. Be patient, and you'll find that this gentle practice can increase your capacity for loving awareness. We are not, after all, trying to change our experience. We are just intending to change our relationship with it.

MEDITATION: Remembering the Body

Take a moment to find your place, a posture that is comfortable and alert. Let the back be straight. Let the head lift. Let your eyes and ears be soft.

Perhaps begin with a few deep, cleansing breaths. Inhale through the nose and exhale through the mouth just a few times before settling into your natural rhythm.

You might take note of your breath. Connect with it. Let your attention gather there for a bit.

Now take a moment to reconnect with your body. How do you feel right now?

There may be areas of tension or pressure. See if you can breathe into those spaces and relax them a bit more.

Take a moment to orient yourself to your body. Imagine your awareness traveling gently down, through your torso and legs and onward to your feet, resting comfortably on the floor. You can pick one foot or broaden your lens to both; either way is fine.

See if you can focus your attention right there, on your feet, for a short while. Start with your big toe; spend a few breaths there, noticing any sensations. Then move to the ball of your foot; pause, breathe, and notice. Now move your attention to the arch, then the heel, then around to the top of the foot, pausing in each spot to let yourself truly experience the sensations arising there right now.

Your mind has probably already started to wander, and that's okay. Just gently acknowledge the thoughts that have arisen before kindly redirecting your attention to your feet. A spirit of curiosity can help: Explore the sensations of your feet, traverse the toes, peek underneath, investigate the presence that they have to offer you.

Let your awareness rise up your body now, noticing as it passes the ankles and into the lower legs, the calves and shins. How does your body feel there? Is there warmth or cool, energy or stillness? Do you feel pressure from your clothing as it may be dangling there?

After pausing for this moment, gently nudge your attention past your knees and into your upper legs, the thighs and hamstrings. These muscles do a lot of work for us throughout the day, powering us around as we walk if we're able. Check in with them now, perhaps offering a kind smile for their efforts.

Moving on, let your attention rise to the middle of the body, the pelvic bowl, the abdomen, the hips. Take note of any unique sensations that arise there.

Nearby we feel our buttocks, perhaps resting on our chair, maybe feeling comfortable or a bit sore. Every possible feeling here can be okay. There's no need to change it. Perhaps lift your attention now to the back, and take in the sensations that are present there.

Moving your concentration around to the belly and chest, pause to notice how they rise and fall with the breath. The belly may feel like a ball, inflating and deflating. In your chest you might notice your heart beating, one of the many organs we depend on so dearly. Let's be here for a moment.

Moving along, you can turn your attention to your arms, elbows, and forearms — your hands, your fingers. Are they activated or at rest? Do they feel stable or unsteady?

Gathering your attention now and bringing it slowly

through the neck and up to the head, what do you notice there? Perhaps your cheeks feel flush, the tip of your nose is cool from the breath, or your jaw is tense or relaxed. Let your attention work its way around your head in this way, giving a brief pause to the sensations that arise there.

Now consider broadening your attention back out to encompass your entire body. Here you are. Right here. Right now. Breathe it in.

Resting comfortably, calm and alert with broad attention, notice if any particular sensation in your body stands out for you now. Perhaps an area of cold or warmth, a tingling, a touch of your skin or the support of the floor.

Just notice that sensation as it arises, as it is, wherever it is. Is it pleasant or unpleasant? Are any emotions associated with it? When you focus on it, does it get stronger or soften? Just acknowledge it. There's no right way to feel.

Stay with this practice for a while, allowing new sensations to arise naturally and turning your focus to them when they do. Let them be as they are, giving them and yourself permission to move on when they pass. You can return to the breath until a new sensation arises.

Here again your mind may wander, doing its thinking thing, the only thing it really knows how to do. That's okay. Just notice, and then gently return your attention to the sensation in your body that's present for you right now.

If a sensation arises that you find challenging to be with — maybe some form of discomfort or pain — consider breathing with it. Let your breath lead you to a sense of stability with whatever it is. It may help to name the sensation with a word: *tightness*, *aching*, *heat*...whatever pops into your mind is the right word. Let it ring in your awareness. Welcome the sensation with your compassionate presence.

In these last few moments, return to your breath, bringing peaceful attention to wherever you feel it. With that awareness, perhaps intend a small bit of gratitude for your body and for this moment you have shared with it.

◆

Please take a moment now to pause and inventory your experience with this practice. This is how we tune in to our body's ever-changing sensations so as to experience the emptiness of the place we inhabit. This process can build our confidence to be with whatever arises. Being truly present here, in this empty place, our connection to all being grows. These walls we have imagined around us begin to fade and we find that, rather than being a container of our experiences, we are just an open door that they pass through. Recognizing the emptiness of our bodies, we no longer feel compelled to hold our experiences inside. We discover that there is truly room for them all. Walt Whitman wrote, "I contain multitudes," echoing the Zen koan: "The worlds of the ten directions will be your total body." When the boundaries between us and our surroundings, between us and all other things, begin to disappear, the true nature of abundance is apparent.

So be your own illumination. Come back to your body and stare at the very nature of reality. There's no veil of concepts in the body; if we look closely, all we see is radical impermanence, infinite possibility. A mysterious dance of energy and motion. There's no center and no boundary. Unless a thought intrudes, no notion of a self can be found.

This realization is the root of our most sacred presence, our truest home, our joyful domicile, our birthright. It is all right here. The truth of our life, our very enlightenment. It's all sitting right here in our body. All we need to do is pay attention.

Chapter 3

Getting to Know Your Mind

Think. Think. Think.
— WINNIE THE POOH

*For subtle realization it is of utmost importance
that you cut off the mind road.*
— ZEN MASTER WU-MEN, *The Gateless Barrier*

Throughout my childhood, I took refuge in the soothing comfort of my thoughts. Confused and pained by what was happening to my family, my mind gave me a seemingly safe and familiar place to hide. I clung to my thoughts, accruing and stacking them like stone blocks in an edifice to protect me from the turmoil unfolding all around. About halfway through college, though, my thoughts turned on me. The wall I had built with them wasn't stone, it was mud. When the rains came, I nearly drowned.

A combination of factors created the storm. During my second year of college, I struggled to transition from my life-changing experience in the simple purity of Nicaragua to the often cruel social hierarchies and stale beer–soaked basements of college life. My self-absorption, a classic symptom of the ego's craving for more, led to a debilitating preoccupation with my peers' opinions of me. The end of a codependent relationship that spring left me feeling isolated, adrift, and unable to rekindle what it felt like to be me. My adolescent journey, with its efforts to find solace in things, places, and my own thoughts, had slowly deprived me of the ability to experience life from the inside out. Now, when I looked in the mirror, I didn't recognize what I saw.

By that summer, during a term that, by tradition, we were required to spend on campus, I was clinically depressed. My bedroom in the old New England fraternity house where I lived lacked air-conditioning, so I struggled to sleep in the July heat. The indifferent sun would pour into my room shortly after 5:00 a.m. as my fraternity brother banged his razor on the sink outside my door before his soccer practice. The gallons of beer I had consumed the night before didn't help. Most mornings I'd lie in bed, essentially unslept, fearing the unhappy hours to come, desperately wondering what they were worth.

If you have experienced depression, then perhaps you can relate to the dull pain I felt, unevenly distributed throughout my body. My thoughts, once crisp and life-affirming, were vague, cluttered, and incoherent, always spiraling downward. Socially, I was frozen, only able to imagine myself through the lens of others' eyes. Seeing myself meant severing from myself, entering others' minds, and voyaging back again to peer at myself. Most of the time, what this perpetual thought cycle projected was an unlikable, unlovable, and unredeemable figment of a person.

Fortunately, I had friends who steadfastly stuck with me

through this difficult time. Even though I wasn't the best wingman, they ballasted me with simple company, journeys to concerts, and bouts of carefree laughter. I had an environmental science teacher who gave me a sympathetic smile and extra time when I slept through the start of my final exam. I had parents whose love and support never wavered. My father saw through my incoherent email ramblings to validate my uniqueness and worth. My mother welcomed me back home at the end of the summer term with her typical unconditional love. She and my stepfather gave me the opportunity to fill the break between the summer and fall terms with exhausting but revitalizing work in his landscaping business. As valuable to me as these specific gestures was the underlying message they conveyed: I was worth helping.

I was also fortunate to have the privilege of access to mental healthcare. During that summer after my sophomore year, I snuck out the side door of my fraternity house every week and hustled across campus to an appointment with a psychiatrist. With his help, I recognized that nothing that had happened to me was in my past. Those experiences were right here, pervading my thoughts and animating my actions like a horde of ghosts shoveling their coal into the engine of my body-mind. If I was going to heal, I needed to reckon with my memories and all the thoughts that accompanied them.

While my depression mercifully subsided, the lifelong journey of understanding my past and reconciling with my thoughts had just begun. Gradually, the Rube Goldberg thought patterns I'd created disentangled, their passageways through the lens of other people's judgments faded, and I was increasingly able to see them for what they were. Only by lessening my attachment to my thoughts could I begin to experience them as facets of my life, not as my life itself. They were not to be feared, but neither could I depend on them for abiding peace. What I slowly realized was that I had lived under their dominion when in fact, all along, I was free.

Freedom with Our Thoughts

Perhaps we all, to some degree, tend to live in our thoughts. We believe we can figure out and resolve our life's challenges with more thinking. We license our thoughts to govern our perceptions and corresponding behaviors. We attach to our thoughts so dearly that we come to think of them as the centerpiece of our lives, supplanting our very selves. We believe that we are our thoughts, that our thoughts are us.

Unfortunately, our thoughts tend to tell us nasty things that, coming from any other source, we would roundly reject: that we don't belong, that the world around us is separate and scarce, that those we encounter are probably a threat, that we are lacking and can only be fulfilled by seeking more (and more). In this mode, we tell ourselves that the person inching forward next to us at the stoplight is our enemy. We fiercely defend our point of view; opposing ones seem like an existential threat to our identity. We believe that we are bad parents, inadequate spouses, and impostor professionals. This is the story of our thought-driven life, and I don't know about you, but for me it has been the norm.

It is never too late to liberate ourselves from these profoundly limiting beliefs and break the chain of these harmful habits of our mind. The opportunity to recognize the true nature of our thoughts and thus the true nature of ourselves is always present. No matter how complex and confused our relationship with our thoughts has become, each new moment offers the unconditional opportunity to put that whole discordant fugue to rest.

What is life like, then? Thoughts and judgments continue to arise, and we continue to acknowledge them, but we recognize them for the simple mind secretions that they are. They may be positive or negative, supportive or damaging, but we are under no obligation to believe them. They have no power of their own to control us, and they certainly are not us. Extricating ourselves from our thoughts in this way, we can then dispense with them as we choose. We can cultivate those that serve us, that resonate with our inner truth, while setting the others aside, letting them pass by as we return to the simple truth of each coming moment. In a life unfiltered by thoughts — the life we are living — we notice that the leaf on the ground in front of us is *green*, that the morning dew under our feet is *wet*, that the sunshine on our brow is *warm*. We can practice letting things be just what they are, including ourselves. This will not stop pain and misfortune from sometimes arising, but everything we experience will be a bit lighter, a bit easier, a bit truer, a bit freer.

Making Thoughts Our Friends or Foes

Only by acknowledging and inquiring into our thoughts can we recognize their emptiness and unravel our limiting preoccupations with them. Casting our gaze on them, we can gradually soften our attachments to them. This gives us the power to remove the thought filter that often stands between us and our lives, allowing us to directly access the vivid radiance of life experience itself.

An important first step is to recognize that thoughts are not our enemy. They have often served us very well, in our lives and over the millennia as our ancestors evolved to become us. The progenitors of our species developed what we now often refer to as the lizard brain, the amygdala that manages our automated functions like breathing and our fight-or-flight response to perceived threats. Thoughts from this region of the brain quickly identified potential predators as we wandered the plains thousands of years ago and still teach us to keep our hand out of the fire.

Later on in the evolutionary process, we developed what is often called the higher brain, or neocortex, which allows us to apply reason and discernment to our experience. After we feel the initial jolt of fear and the instinct to fight or flee, for example, when an unfamiliar dog surprises us with loud barks, these are the kinds of thoughts that remind us it's probably best to stay calm and extend our hand gently. This portion of the brain also allows us to imagine and create, to calm and soothe ourselves. Our thoughts, whatever region of our brain they come from, can be beneficial.

The challenges arise when we unconditionally believe that our thoughts are the truth, that they are the food instead of the menu. We float along living in them rather than in our lives. How many times have we walked into a room and forgotten why we're there? How often do we drive, eat, or bathe while concentrating on something entirely different?

It is particularly problematic that our evolutionary training and its dedication to survival have conspired to give us an extreme negativity bias — we have needed to be able to spot danger before all else to survive. We don't just tend to believe our thoughts; we prioritize and favor the negative ones. You may have had a birthday party as a youngster that was a joyful experience. One friend didn't include you in the next round of the video game, though, or your parent directed a crisp word at you for spilling your soda, and that is probably the only thing you remember. A 95 percent positive experience thus exists today in your mind as an exclusively negative one.

This negativity bias can form toxic loops in which our thoughts and actions symbiotically reinforce our false beliefs about ourselves. Because we are prone to correlate our thoughts with our identity, few things are more threatening to us than the possibility that we are wrong. We believe this so deeply that we often behave in ways we know are harmful as subconscious affirmations of our self-loathing. Then, when the consequence of that action comes due, we see it as validation of that underlying untrue thought about ourselves.

For example, if I believe (as I often do) the thought that I am a bad parent, I might tell myself that I need to be stricter about an aspect of my child's behavior — playing a video game for too long, leaving a mess of crumbs in the back seat of the car, or neglecting their homework. In this state of mind, I am much more prone to snap at my child, raise my voice, and shame them in a way that is harmful to them, not to mention utterly ineffective at altering the behavior in question. I have also harmed myself; I lie in bed that night regretting my outburst, torturing myself for being a bad parent, and grieving my innocent child's tears. Thus my behavior has validated my underlying negative thought, hardening the neural pathways that connect the two, and reinforced my habituated response. "See? I was right!" my mind tells itself.

The Emptiness of Thoughts

To deepen our inquiry into the nature of thought, we will ratchet down the microscope on them one more click. What are they, really? Why do we choose to give them so much power over our lives?

The basic neurological building blocks of our thoughts are neurons. Our brains have more than 100 billion of these cells that transmit tiny pieces of information (in the form of molecules called neurotransmitters), ranging from your perception of the shape of the letters on this page to your interpretation of the ideas they represent. They have treelike features called axons that send this information across connections between them called synapses.

Why am I giving you this mini lecture in neuroscience? It is so that you can see that there is in fact no demarcated location in three-dimensional space that we can point to and define it as a thought. Each of the seventy thousand thoughts you will have today is comprised of thousands of tiny cells, their atomic components, and their channels of communication. Which one makes it a thought? That whiff you just caught of your morning coffee that traveled through the nerve endings in your nose and into your mind and then translated its sensory textures and feeling tones to define your experience of it — what is that, again?

Moreover, thoughts, and the combination of them that we call our mind, have no known headquarters, no captain's chair that directs and organizes them. As Yongey Mingyur

Rinpoche explores in *The Joy of Living*, neuroscience has abandoned the search for a conductor of the symphony of our mind. What we call *mind* can more aptly be thought of as a jazz performance, with each thought spontaneously improvised, a "perpetually evolving *event*, rather than a distinct entity." If we peel back all the layers, thoughts have no core to call their own.

We can also understand the emptiness of thoughts through the lens of impermanence. We know from our experience that they continuously arise and fall. Some linger for a few moments; some vanish almost as soon as they arise. Perhaps you've experienced redirecting a child's attention from the cookie on the counter toward the bouncy red ball in a corner of the room. See how easily their attention turns and how quickly the thought of the cookie fades away? Our minds continue to act this way throughout our lives. One moment we are trying to focus on our breath, the next we are imagining what we'll have for breakfast. One moment we are changing the radio station in the car, the next we're reacting to the changing stoplight ahead.

Thoughts that have a longer lifespan also reveal the ever-renewing nature of impermanence. Our thoughts and ideas about our job and friends, our memories, and our beliefs take on new tones each time we revisit them. Even the stickiest of thoughts, that "greatest hits tape" that seems so difficult to turn off when we wake up in the middle of the night, changes every time. What's at the top of your chart? Maybe "I need to change my job"? "I have no idea how I'm going to complete that assignment today"? "Ooh, I wish I'd gotten in this extra burn during that argument last week"?

At the same time, thoughts are empty in the sense that they are conditioned on an infinite array of precursors and causes. With a memory, for example, there was the incident such as it was, our experience of it through our five senses, our interpretation of those perceptions, and our judgments and attendant considerations of how it relates to the broader context of our lives. Without each of these, the memory would not be what it is, but which elements make it the memory we have?

As we explore these considerations, our view of our thoughts might begin to change. Instead of the lasting, concrete, powerful forces to which we assign the truth of our lives, we might begin to see them as temporary, ever-changing, dispersed, empty features of our experience. We can choose which ones to believe and cultivate the ones that serve us. As for the rest, we are utterly free in each moment to let them pass through. Let's practice, then, our exercise of that freedom.

REFLECTION: Taking Inventory of Your Thoughts

Perhaps get out some pen and paper. We are going to start simply. Just write down your thoughts as they are happening right now, characterizing them however each thought warrants. It might be something like "This table is brown." "The air in the room is cool." "I'm hungry." "What's the point of this exercise?" There's no need to filter or judge here. Just let the thoughts pour forth as they do. Continue with this for a few minutes, just allowing the passageways of your mind to unfold on your page.

After you are satisfied that you have given your thoughts

adequate exploration — maybe you have filled up a page or so — take a pause and observe what you have written. Do some of the thoughts relate to what is physically present for you here and now, specific and concrete? Are others more like reflections or ruminations on what you are experiencing, abstract and general? How many relate to the past? How many look to the future? How many have a positive tone? How many are less pleasant? Most likely, what you've written includes a combination of these and other potential categorizations.

Don't worry, there is no scoring this exercise; no points are going to be awarded for better thoughts or deducted for worse ones. We are just starting to take the first step of noticing our thoughts. We are turning toward them to get a better look at their contours, textures, and hues, the things that make each thought undefinably unique. Like snowflakes on the slope, grains of sand on the beach, or stars in the sky, an unimaginable array of thoughts is always coming forth in our minds. On the one hand, they are extremely ordinary. On the other, they are awe-inspiring constellations of our human experience. Every single one — bright or faded, happy or sad — is a precious, passing miracle.

Attachment to Thoughts

Thoughts are the quintessential source of our attachments and an excellent means of understanding this Buddhist concept. We can be attached to a place we like to visit, a friend who supports us, or a collection we enjoy accruing. Underneath all these, though, is our attachment to our thoughts about them. Usually, our experience is not so much about that place, person, or thing; it is about our judgments and preferences about them, our memories, attitudes, and expectations. Likewise, we attach to thoughts about ourselves, the stories we hold to explain who we are, why we do what we do, and what we hope to become.

A key to experiencing this is to notice that almost everything we encounter and every thought we experience has a positive or negative tone. We probably find each thought, to some degree, pleasant or unpleasant. Fueled by our evolutionary survival training, if something is pleasant for us, we instinctually want more of it or fear that it will go away. If it is unpleasant, we fear it will continue or wish it would go away. Wanting and craving, fear and aversion — these are the two sides of the coin of attachment. Whichever we are experiencing, what is missing is the object of our attention just as it is, before we apply these judgments. We drag a clouded image of that thing along with us into the next moment. Our thoughts become an obstacle to our authentic experience.

Consider the people you know. Is it possible to call them to mind without arousing attitudes about them as positive or negative, without thinking about whether you'd like to see them again soon or whether you'd rather avoid them? Maybe this attitude shifts as you look at the person from a different angle and see a different aspect of them. Either way, if we are human, judgment is probably part of the picture, and we hold on to these judgments as vital to our experience of that person. In this way, we are attached to our thoughts; we can see this wherever we turn, about whatever we are thinking. In the most extreme form, we are so attached to our thoughts that we believe they *are* us.

The soil from which such attachments arise is our

underlying belief that these thoughts, like the things around us, are separate from us. We can only crave or fear something if we believe it has an independent identity from us that remains fixed and defined. In other words, we believe that our thoughts, like the piece of artwork on the wall or the chair under us, is "over there," that we are over here, and that never the twain shall meet. But as we explored above, what aspect of a thought gives it the sustained identity or selfhood that we ascribe to it? Search as you might, I wager heavily that you will never find it. It is comprised of too many different things, from too many different times, always changing in too many ways, for us to pinpoint a certain feature that makes a thought what it is. In that way, while our thoughts are not us, they are not separate from us. For each empty thought, what is there to crave or fear?

We will explore this in more detail in the next chapter when we consider the consequence of these attachments: suffering. For now, perhaps you can begin to see again the ongoing theme of this book: By pausing to remember the underlying emptiness of things, we can relax and ultimately abandon our attachment to them, the overlay of our attitudes and judgments. Recognizing thoughts this way prevents them from maintaining their power over us. Suddenly they are at our disposal, to use or dispense as serves us best. Our grip on the features of our lives begins to loosen, and we are free, buoyantly able to respond to the ever-changing waves.

The Art of Lessening Thoughts

The art of lessening has nothing to do with "just letting it go" or otherwise turning away from our experience. To sunder the bonds of attachment that drive us into a state of reactivity, the essential practice is to turn toward. In doing so, we transform our obstacles and distractions into gateways to freedom and joy.

With thoughts, the first step is to acknowledge they are there. When you observe a thought, you might simply note, "I am thinking." This statement is always true. In reading the words on this page, in forming your judgments about these ideas, in sensing the lights and colors in your room, you are thinking. So acknowledge that. There's nothing wrong with it.

As we notice the content of our thoughts, we can acknowledge their flavor. For example, typical thoughts may include sensing, planning, or remembering. If we look closely, we might also see that they have an emotional hue, such as regret, worry, or criticism. It can be very helpful to name our thoughts to ourselves this way so that we can more clearly acknowledge our awareness of them. Even as we simply acknowledge, we are exercising our muscle to be with whatever is arising for us.

A helpful analogy often used in Buddhist circles is that of a waterfall. The gushing water is the stream of thoughts running through our head. Instead of being immersed in the deluge pouring over the cliff or drowning in the swirling water below, we can stand on a ledge near the water, safely watching it as it rushes by. In doing so, we acknowledge that our thoughts are part of our experience but that they are not us; we do not have to let them control us.

Another important step in the art of lessening thoughts is to resist the natural tendency to judge. If we are fearful of a future event, for example, we might be inclined to condemn ourselves for worrying too much. We might get frustrated that, despite our efforts to practice mindfulness, we still get caught in this loop of anxious thoughts. These judgments are the "second arrow" — the added suffering we create when we judge how we experience things.

For me the metaphor that is even more apt is that of a boomerang that keeps flying, dinging us each time it passes by. We might notice that, as we apply our judgments to our thoughts, we compound their intensity and transform them into emotions. The emotions evoke new judgments, and again and again we invite the boomerang to hit us.

Here we can see the interrelationship between thoughts and emotions. Some traditions and practices parse them, but they are so intertwined that, for me, it is simplest to address them similarly. Just as each thought has innumerable causes and conditions that spawned it, underlying each emotion are countless thoughts and judgments. If we closely examine an emotion in the way we have other objects of our experience, we may discover that it lacks clear edges, vanishes as quickly as it arose, and is bereft of any inherent feature that makes it what it is. Emotions are absolutely real, often very painfully so, and they are also empty.

As with thoughts, if we proceed with this practice of lessening, we can begin to see emotions more clearly and expand our capacity to be with them in a freer and more peaceful way. We can pause to acknowledge that an emotion has arisen and then name it. In that simple two-step process, we have already begun to soften its power over us and decrease the probability that we will slip into a reactive state. We may begin to notice some of our own greatest hits and, rather than resist them, open ourselves to being with them in a new way: "Hello, regret, my old friend, here you are again."

Reversing the Tide of Attachment

As we take another step along the path of lessening, it can be helpful to apply a bit of skepticism to our thoughts and emotions to help rebalance a lifetime (genetically, millennia) of ceding our power to them. Thoughts and emotions by themselves are not good or bad, but they can be wrong. Once we reconsider them from a sturdier vantage point, we can see that they are almost always either incomplete or overblown, lacking important details or including false or irrelevant ones, and heavily shaded by our own biases. And that's just for starters. At the very least, we can rest assured that, even as we acknowledge our thoughts and emotions, we are not obligated to believe them.

For practice, call to mind a thought you maintain about yourself or someone you know well, perhaps an unpleasant one like "I'm a little lazy" or "That friend is flaky." Whatever pops up for you quickly will work fine. Notice that the belief invariably carries some kind of emotional hue, an extra layer of baggage attached to it that usually includes a notion that the situation should be different. Then you might start to regret your tendency to judge. The boomerang is heading your way.

To help anchor your authentic experience of this belief, notice how it feels in your body. Take a few breaths to be with your sensory experience of it. Now get curious about that thought. Consider asking some of these questions:

"Is it always true? Am I so sure?"

"Is it possible another person might disagree with me about it? What valid objections might they raise?"

"Am I obligated to believe this thought? Who or what is enforcing that obligation on me? Why am I giving them that power?"

Pivoting, you might now ask:

"What would it be like if I didn't believe this thought?"

"What kind of person would I be if I didn't believe it?"

"How would I be in relationship with others if I didn't believe it? How would my behavior change?"

"What would it feel like right now if I simply stop believing it?"

Check in with your body. How do you feel? Keep breathing. Has anything about your relationship with this thought changed, even if only slightly or briefly? What was it like to suspend your belief in this thought for a moment?

As we practice lessening our thoughts in this way, we may find more balance with the waves that otherwise toss us around. When situations arise that prompt intense emotions — the ones when we are apt to fire off an angry text, yell, or just shut down — we might more often pause and reconsider these underlying thoughts that we are so determined to believe. In doing so, we continue to expand our capacity to be with our experiences and offer even our negative emotions some peace and equanimity. We can continue that dialogue with our old friend, regret: "Thanks for your visit. Safe travels as you move along your way."

In conclusion, it's important to revisit where we started: The purpose of this practice is not to deny the reality of your thoughts or your perfectly valid experience of them. The art of lessening is not about avoiding or dismissing thoughts and emotions. The appropriate response to a sad event is to be sad. When something sad arises for you, please, be sad. These experiences are a precious part of your life.

What might change is our relationship to them. Gradually, thoughts and emotions lose their power over us. As they soften, we can reacquaint ourselves with life itself, the thing that is awaiting us after all the boomeranging thoughts are put to rest. The blade of grass — its texture and smell, its shifting hue depending on its age — is so much more beautiful and interesting than our thoughts about it. This is the opportunity that our thoughts present: Once we start to disentangle our *selves* from them, we can awaken to the present moment with more clarity and freedom. As Zen master and poet Wu-Men wrote:

Ten thousand flowers in spring, the moon in autumn,
a cool breeze in summer, snow in winter.
If your mind isn't clouded by unnecessary things,
this is the best season of your life.

MEDITATION: Greeting Empty Thoughts

Take a moment to find your seat. Wherever suits you for some dedicated practice is fine. Perhaps you are in a chair or on a cushion on the floor. Let yourself settle into this space.

Allow yourself to feel at home. You can close your eyes if you feel comfortable doing so, or you can leave them dimly open.

Consider the sensations arising in your body right now. Are there any areas of obvious tension or discomfort? See if you can relax them a bit more. Let your heart be soft. Let its natural kindness open you to what is arising.

Now notice the fact that you are breathing. Connect with your breath and its rhythm without making any effort to change it. Perhaps feel the movement of your body in response.

Are any sounds arising for you right now? Take note of what you're hearing. What's coming into your ears? There's no need to go out and grab the sounds. Just let them come to you and find out what's there.

Turning your attention to your mind now, you might begin by counting your thoughts. Staying connected with your breath and body, just noticing each time a different thought bubble pops up. It might be something like "There's pressure on my foot," or "The air in the room is cool," or "I'm going to eat a sandwich after this." Whatever they are, note each one with a simple count. You are standing on the ledge by the waterfall, letting it rush by. Just stay here for a while, counting.

Peering more closely, let yourself focus on a prominent thought that's arising for you right now. Give yourself a moment to pinpoint one for reflection. You can stabilize your gaze by gently naming the type of thought it is: sensing, planning, remembering, worrying. Let the naming be just a soft whisper in the back of your mind.

Consider whether this thought is part of a recurring

theme. Are you remodeling your house again, recycling an old argument, or planning your afternoon? You can acknowledge this with a simple, "Hello again, I know you."

If any emotional charges are traveling with your thought, you can notice them too. Maybe consider whether the thought is pleasant or unpleasant. More complicated emotions may be coming up as well: frustration or sadness or perhaps a sense of levity or joy. Maybe right now there's not much to feel, or the emotions are hard to identify. Just notice that. Perhaps you are experiencing a sense of disconnectedness or numbness. That's also a fine way to feel right now.

Whatever it is, let yourself be curious about this thought. Are any feelings in your body arising along with it? Has the rhythm of your breath changed as you focus on it? Taking another step closer, maybe ask, "Am I sure this thought is true? Do I have to believe it?"

As you explore this thought, perhaps you experience a sense of stillness and spaciousness. The thought is gently orbiting in your attention as you sit peacefully by. Or, just as likely, the notion of this thought has you racing down a busy road, scribbling paragraphs about it in your mind. Whichever the case may be, just notice that.

As you give this thought your kind attention, how does it respond? Does it change? Soften or strengthen? Just notice that too. There's no need to change how you are thinking. Right now, you are just a witness.

After you've given this thought its due, gently return your attention to your breath for a moment to recenter yourself. Take a break inside the breath.

As new thoughts arise, just continue to give them your

attention with curiosity and kindness. Notice if they arouse any sensations in your body. You can give them a soft label, as we've practiced, before you let them fade away. After each thought passes, you can simply return to focusing on your breath until a new thought arises.

Continue with this practice for a while, observing your thoughts as they arise and fall.

"Hello, new thought. What do you have to say? Thank you. Farewell."

Notice, if you might, the space between thoughts. Imagine you are an open sky with thoughts floating through like clouds. You might allow a faint smile to curl your lips.

In these final moments, just rest in the mindful awareness of your thoughts, new or old, foreign or familiar. Here you are in your seat, and here they are arising with you. However you feel, perhaps appreciate that you are gradually becoming gentler, freer, and more open.

✦

After you have completed this practice, check in with yourself on how it went. You might note how this practice gives you permission to acknowledge your thoughts. Too many of us have misunderstood mindfulness or meditation to be about eliminating them. But that is exactly wrong. The Ten-Verse Kannon Sutra of Timeless Life, a central Buddhist text, says this: "Thought after thought arises in mind. Thought after thought is not separate from mind. Each moment itself is mind."

Even the great sages of ancient times recognized that thoughts will always arise. Trying to stop them is like trying to stop the wind; it is only going to cause us frustration. While they are not who we are, they are also not separate from us, something we need to fear or control, crave or avoid. We do not need to believe in them as if they constitute the reality of our lives. What a relief!

You may have encountered another facet of thoughts. I was guiding a class through this meditation recently when a curious thing happened. In the discussion that followed, several students described their experience when I invited them to focus on a specific thought for further investigation. What they discovered was that there was no thought to be found; the concerted effort to locate and maintain a thought seemed to cause the thoughts to scramble, fade, or disappear entirely. This helped me remember just how delicate and impermanent our thoughts actually are, despite our preoccupation with them.

This practice of allowing yourself to acknowledge thoughts while maintaining your heart center with your breath will help you cultivate a spaciousness and peace even as the stream of thoughts flows by. As we watch them rise and fall, over and over, they start to lose their power. Ideas that once felt indelible begin to fade; our attachments to them weaken. As we pay closer and closer attention, their emptiness shines through, brighter and brighter. Though they always have a spot on the stage, they are no longer the star of the show.

Chapter 4

Actualizing Your Work

*In the mind harmonious with the Way... all striving
is quieted;... all is empty, lucid, and self-illuminating.
There is no exertion, no waste of energy.*

— Seng Ts'an, *On Faith in Mind*

*We thought of life by analogy with a journey, with a pilgrimage
which had a serious purpose at the end.... But we missed the point
the whole way along. It was a musical thing and you were
supposed to sing or dance while the music was being played.*

— Alan Watts, "The Hoax"

After graduating from college, I bought into the uniquely American religion that worships work as a core source of meaning in our lives. "If you aren't growing, you're dying," says the traditional business coach, pithily capturing the ethos of more-ness. I followed that principle throughout my career to a T.

At the law firm where I got started, the ultimate badge of success was getting the "opportunity" to do more work. Ambition is voracious, hungrily consuming tasks and earning more of them as the reward. I loved how my billable hours log absorbed the wet blue ink of my pen. I would look at the smeared full page at the end of the day with great satisfaction, an emblem of my industriousness. I'd get a call from a partner's office and beam with pride as I sped off for a new assignment. Staying busy was work at its best. Downtime, gaps in my calendar, opportunities to pause for friendly conversation at the coffeepot: those were indicia of failure.

I gravitated to health policy, serving briefly as an aide to a US Senate committee. Western medicine is an epic demonstration of the more-ness ethos. Its solution to every illness is more — more tests, more procedures, more treatment, more spending. That pursuit of more-ness translated into my daily life.

As a Senate staffer, I observed — and willfully participated in — a culture of competition. At our best, we competed with our ideas, and at our worst with our stature and ego. Even among those of us in the same political party, it felt like our primary purpose was to advance our identities through our career ambitions rather than to embrace our collective wisdom and energy. We were all there to do good, I believe, but we were often quite nasty and unhappy about it. We issued ultimatums and stormed out of the room; we secretly convened subversive working groups; we jabbed each other with polished DC snark.

Later, I built a career as a consultant, with intense focus on generating clients and accruing wealth. Primarily motivated by fear of reprising my father's mistakes, I was constantly anxious in this place of never-enough-ness. Every time a client asked to speak to me, I feared they planned to terminate our contract. Every time a colleague or employee asked for a meeting,

I worried they were harboring a stinging complaint about me. I found it difficult to maintain partnerships, always underestimating the other's contribution and suspecting they were doing the same with mine. Many of my days in DC were spent running around Capitol Hill, my mind always gazing away from the moment and ahead to my sunset gratitude meditation of choice: a triple martini with olives.

While I was fortunate, and am grateful, to have found some material success, I am still counting the personal costs — the debts I accrued those years achieving this "success" I dreamed of. I wake up at night to a vision of my three-year-old daughter, her tiny pink fingers splayed on the window by our front door, crying for me not to leave our Denver home for yet another flight to Washington. Diverting my gaze, I hustle down the steps toward the awaiting taxi, taking refuge in the hum of its engine. Sighing to the driver, I beg him to speed away as quickly as possible — away from the tenderness of this moment and toward the more-ness of my work.

Often my kids would get back from school in the middle of my home-based workday. They'd come running with their gently pattering footsteps to my office door, eager to initiate our routine playtime before dinner, hoping we'd build a fort in the shabby blue sofa downstairs or chase each other around the small patch of green grass in our backyard.

All too often, I greeted their precious entreaties with a shrill *"I'm on the phone!"* my arms swaying in frantic dismissal, their faces retreating behind the oak office door. Didn't they understand I was doing something important? Couldn't they respect me and all that I was earning for them?

I began to realize that what they really understood and respected was our time together, the gentle love we shared. That was, after all, the ultimate purpose for my work: to secure time and space for connecting with the people I care about. But I was too attached to my identity of output to see that this path of more-ing had led me far astray from this core intention.

My attachment to work also blinded me to the true possibility of my daily experience. Each task was an obstacle to be tackled and crossed off my ever-replenishing to-do list. Meanwhile, I was learning new details about this complex and ever-evolving field, often engaging in conversations with insightful and passionate people and frequently able to travel to new places. Only later did I come to appreciate that, whatever the purpose of my task, I could be with my experience with joy and presence.

Beautifully Empty Work

Seeing through the dogma of more-ness is key to awakening to the truth of our work. Rather than rejecting work (aversion being another form of attachment), what if we could be with it in a different way? What if we could see the bits of material reality that comprise our workday and career path for the simple shards of existence that they are, arising ever so briefly in each instant — real, fascinating, empty.

Imagine your workday as wading through a stream, chest deep. You're splashed by the water and swayed by the current; the rocks beneath your feet alternate between jagged and slippery; the fish and vegetation bump into or around you. Mired here, you can't see your circumstances in their simple beauty;

you're likely resisting its discomforts and lunging toward its pleasantries, if not just hurrying to the other side altogether.

Realizing the emptiness of work allows you to walk on the water. You're still there, still present, still working, but you're free from the push and pull of the torrent. You can see clearly all that's arising, but it can't attach to you, nor you to it. Each thing passes through in its time as you walk steadily on.

What does this look like in the context of our daily lives? Maybe, like me, you have awakened with anxiety about the mountain of work facing you that day. Perhaps you've felt yourself hustling from one task to the next in a fearful, defensive posture, with each to-do a projectile aimed in your direction that you must swiftly bat away. Maybe you suffer tense conversations with bosses or colleagues and then revisit your incompletely phrased fragments repeatedly into the night. That's wading in the stream, wet and muddy.

At other times, you wake up with some passion and excitement for your work. Maybe you can imagine greeting each new email and phone call as a morsel of your unique and improbable life; maybe you can feel equipped to respond to them with your truest self. Maybe you can be at ease in that difficult conversation, free to honor the other person with your listening and to respond with integrity. Perhaps there's space for creativity, even joy, in your tasks.

This is the workday you deserve; it's the career that is your birthright. And you can make it so by realizing its emptiness.

REFLECTION: Your Experience of Work

Take a moment to pause here and reflect on your career and your work. Perhaps you are on the downhill slope, approaching retirement or already there. Perhaps you are staring at the mountain ahead, most of your work so far having been in school.

Consider your personal, embodied experience of this work. How does it usually feel to wake up and envision your day ahead? What is it like to take your seat at your desk, your laptop, your service counter, your post? Is your mind with you, attending to the work, or is it somewhere else? The invitation is to just let in the truth of your experience, without judgment. Whatever it is, there is always an opportunity for you to deepen your fulfillment with whatever you are doing.

In the sections and practices ahead, we will explore teachings and methods for reconnecting with your work in a fresh and enlivening way.

Suffering at Work

Buddhist teachings about suffering can help us see through our attachment to work and the dogma of perpetual accumulation. The Four Noble Truths are the Buddha's foundational teaching, providing a framework for all Buddhist thought. The First Noble Truth of Buddhism is "All is suffering." Maybe this resonates with you, or maybe it sounds like an incredibly dour way to get started. It takes a little unpacking to realize the beauty of this simple observation.

Some people understand the Noble Truth of suffering as only pertaining to the "bad" things in life: physical or emotional pain, the passing of loved ones, our own mortality. We might fall into that interpretation if we just look at the beginning of the Buddha's story — the part where he leaves his cloistering palace walls to witness, for the first time, sickness, old age, and death. But we're not just talking about pain or unpleasantness here.

A better translation of the term *suffering* is "unsatisfactoriness." So the First Noble Truth of suffering is better put this way: Everything is ultimately unsatisfactory, even the "good" stuff like the promotion at work or a sunny day.

Why? Why are all things ultimately unsatisfactory? For starters, because they do not last, they cannot last, no matter how hard we cling to them. Our attachment can never be fulfilled. As we explored in the previous chapter, we instinctively regard every aspect of our experience as pleasant or unpleasant. That thing — an idea, a memory, a piece of clothing, an assignment from our boss — is something we either want more of or we want to avoid. That's craving or aversion — in other words, attachment.

My first Zen teacher encapsulated this principle in words I'll always remember. I had giggled uncomfortably through my first yoga and meditation experience with my high school friends. Afterward, Master Adam pulled us aside on the sidewalk and said, in his crisp staccato cadence, "When someone says 'Oh, you look handsome,' you feel happy. But then someone says, 'Oh, you look scummy,' and you feel sad."

It's really that simple. A quick turn of phrase can leave us attached, either chasing a positive feeling or fleeing a negative one. In this state of reactivity, we're responding without really noticing. It's exhausting. Caught in it, we will never be satisfied, because that thing we are resisting or craving isn't actually what we think it is. We treat a kind or cruel comment like it has a sustained, inherent character that's separate from us, presenting to us as either supportive or threatening.

But when we take a closer look, we might see that this thing or idea that we're attached to, like all things, lacks any element that gives it a coherent identity. It's a temporary confluence of innumerable different components and preconditions: the state of mind of the person making the comment, our own mood, our clothing, the condition of our hair, the time and place of the encounter, and so on. That comment also arose ever so briefly, unique to its time and place, lacking any ability of its own to exist into the future. Anything we ascribe to it beyond that is just the workings of our imagination. In and of itself, it is empty.

This gap between the empty reality of things — a comment, our business card, the email in front of us, our thoughts about the next task — and our perception of them as harboring a persistent, separate identity is the reason we can never be satisfied by them. We are attaching to something that isn't there. You cannot feed a hungry ghost, they say. We can't be quenched by an illusion. So, unsatisfied, we suffer.

You may be surprised to hear that it is in fact by embracing this emptiness that we can find true, lasting fulfillment. Why? Because when we are no longer attached to illusions, we are free to engage with each moment with genuine presence, vigor, and ease. The unattached mind is the clearest mind, the most creative, the most capable of navigating challenges. It is awed by and grateful for whatever arises.

Attached to the illusion, we are preoccupied with the pointed email we just received from our boss, lost in speculation about their motivations and judgments. Dreaming only of the outcome of our work, material or otherwise, we are bringing only a fraction of ourselves to the task at hand, the work we have arrived at that moment to address.

Recognizing the Emptiness of Work

How do we identify emptiness and use that insight about it to cultivate a new relationship with our laptop, our productivity dashboard, the Zoom conference screen, and the next moment to come? Travel with me to your workday. Visualize yourself in the office, at your desk, on the factory line, or at the espresso machine. I'm going to explore a specific example, but you are invited to translate it to your typical working environment.

At the age of forty-four, I found myself standing at the food-prep station on the opening day of the alcohol-free bar I founded. Rather than feeling joyful and exhilarated by the packed house and line of customers streaming out the front door, relishing this dream that had become reality, I was trembling. Facing a pile of order tickets, the staff and I were overwhelmed. The packaging of the various deli meats and cheeses we used to prepare a charcuterie board were greasy and difficult to open. The olive jar was spilling. The plates were blemished. A waiter came back begging for an overdue order. I overheard a customer's frustration about our untrained and disorganized service. I felt shame, embarrassment, fear. I had fully invested myself into this passion project and exposed myself to the incessant judgment of Yelp reviews, online chatrooms, and social media comment threads. I was afraid our failures that day would doom the business, lay to waste my investment of time and resources, and embarrass me and my family. My stomach was tight, my jaw clenched, my voice oscillating between meekly timid and aggressively demanding. Everything and everyone around me was a threat. All I wanted was to make it through the next moment, and for the damn salami package to finally open.

What if I had experienced that moment differently? We can start with any detail. It doesn't matter if it seems foolishly mundane; it's a perfect representation of the whole of our experience. That's the beauty of emptiness. It's not a void that consumes our sense of meaning; it's the essential element of every syllable of being, the thing that unites each and every thing that ever was and will be. Everything is exquisitely unique, poetically ephemeral, and eternally unblemished. Sometimes we just need to open ourselves up to seeing a point of entry into this timeless home.

Back at the bar, I am literally clinging to this ladle of kalamata olives that I'm trying to delicately pour into this one-inch-wide tin cup. I'm fixated on it in that moment, in all of its oily drips and fumbles, as the cause of my suffering, the tip of the iceberg of underlying emotions ensconced in my body and mind. If I can take a single, fully embodied breath, however, this emblem of fear and anxiety offers me a portal to ease and equanimity. No longer the cause of my suffering, it is my gateway to liberation.

To answer its beckoning call, I might consider: Where did these olives come from? What fields produced beautiful trees bearing their fruit when the perfect season sprouted its bounty? Whose labor harvested them? How far did they travel from their home on the earthbound tree to their assemblage in an unctuous vat and onward to packaging? What about the kind food representative who helped create our menu and cheerfully delivered our below-the-minimum order each week?

And the olives themselves? Take that one that just splashed into its new home in the serving cup. It's defined by its sleekness, its bruised purple hues, its penetrating smell. All these relative aspects arise together, right now, as "olive." Empty as can be, the olive is just a temporary aggregate of infinite possibilities — all that its components have ever been and ever will become. Arising anew in this moment, yes, it is unique — exquisite, miraculous. But underneath it all is its elegant emptiness, the being that remains in the absence of all our sensation, perception, and judgment. That's the thing that unites this one slippery olive with it all. That's what binds it and me and all time together.

The olive isn't just the source of my fear and frustration. Beneath that is my ambition, my identification with the path that brought me to that stressful moment and has me antic-ipating its forthcoming fate. What's that made of? It's built on handwritten brainstormed legal pads and business plan software, Google reviews and receipts, inspiring team meet-ings and confrontational ones, inventory days and Facebook ads. What is this ambition? What is this identity I've woven into this instant I have in the company of a kalamata olive? It is completely empty, lacking any inherent nature of its own, arising in that particular way so briefly in that moment. Like everything else, the olive offered a mirror to view my notion of an ego self and allowed me to see there was nothing there.

If I'd had the wherewithal in that moment to realize this, how would things have changed? All the details would be the same, but my experience of them could have been radically different. As I visualize myself submerging into the cleansing cold plunge of emptiness, a smile is already creeping onto my lips. The fragile ego that was facing an existential threat is replaced by the immutable presence of all being that can never be blemished. My trembling begins to ease, my stomach begins to relax into the ebb and flow of the breath. Emptying the moment has taken with it the trivialities that conspired to deny me my right to be present in my life as it truly is, as I truly am.

What a privilege to be there, with that olive, making a board of tasty meats, cheeses, and vegetables for some stranger to enjoy? Look at all these employees who trusted me enough to take a job in this weird start-up, hustling around in their way, manifesting themselves with their truest intentions. The music I'd carefully selected for this special event cracks back through my denying veneer — Thom Yorke's voice soars over the clanking plates; the rhythm of my movement starts to align with Green Day's power chords.

If I had just paused in this moment of awareness, the weight of all those hours planning and preparing, and also the uncertainty ahead, could simply lift. They aren't here anymore now. I'm not bound by them. I'm actually free to be here in this moment just as I am. What comes forth then is ease, gratitude, curiosity, maybe even some awe and a side of joy. The elements of reality are still there for me to contend with: I need to get this order moving; I want our customers to have an enjoyable experience; I'd like to give this social enterprise my best effort. How much better to approach these tasks with this new mindset, this place of wholeness and inherent satisfaction? Nothing has changed, and everything has changed. The plate is served. The next order arrives.

REFLECTION: Enter into Your Work

What emblem of your workday challenges can you imagine at this moment? It can be an object, a task, a thought, a preoccupation with some event, past or future. It doesn't really matter what it is, as long as you can bring it to life now with texture.

Spend some time recognizing how your body reacts to your experience of it. As you bring it to mind, check in with your sensations: Are you relaxed or tense, is your breathing shallow or deep, is your mind calm or scrambled? Let the rhythm of your breath help connect you to this moment and a clearer view of the item you have chosen to focus on.

Consider: What are its material features, whether ink on a page, glowing pixels on a screen, or neurons firing in your brain? What are its origins? Everything is born out of innumerable causes. What preconditions contributed to the arising of this experience you have called to mind? Perhaps there was cultivation of natural resources, manufacturing, a series of conversations, evolutions of relationships, each contributing person's history, mindset, and actions. Go ahead and let your mind explore these many paths for a while.

Calling all these elements to the fore, what then is left of the original object or experience you have identified? Is it really just the label and judgments you have applied to it? What aspect of it makes it so and only so? Is your mind open to the possibility that this thing is in fact a temporary manifestation of infinite possibilities? Can you really trace the path that led to it being here or that it will follow into the future? Can you crack the veneer of your mind's tendency to categorize such things so swiftly as beneficial or threatening, something to be accrued or avoided?

As we have been doing in our ongoing practice, see if you can pause before rushing in with answers to these questions. We want to expand our capacity to be with these uncertainties. Gradually, as you practice these pauses amid the tempest of your work, you may find that your attachment to what arises will soften and your freedom and ease with these moments will strengthen — and you may begin to find a fulfillment that you have never known before.

A Hard Case

In exploring these mindfulness-based techniques and Buddhist ideas, it can be challenging to understand how they apply to the most difficult situations: the existential threat to our job, the deterioration of our ambitious goals, or the harm we have caused (or that has been done to us) in the past. I have come to believe, though, that these situations are exactly where this practice is most important. They are not counterexamples; rather, they are precisely the perfect place to cultivate our kind awareness.

During a recent class at the Zen Center of Denver, a student shared about her extremely stressful trajectory with a start-up. As she led it through a phase of rapid expansion, growing the staff from a few to several dozen, her stress and anxiety were so severe that she began to experience panic attacks. For months, she had them daily. To manage this, she began deepening her mindfulness practice and, while still passionately pursuing her work, lessening her attachment to her judgments and corresponding distress about them. Now (the same day as one of our classes), after all that effort and sacrifice, she was just handed the responsibility of laying off over half the employees and, perhaps, preparing for the dissolution of the company.

The student shared that, thanks to her practice over the preceding years, she was able to recognize that the emptiness — of her preconceived ideas about how this experience should unfold, of the interactions and tasks and hardware that comprised this endeavor — created space for her worst fears and anxieties to pass through. It is because of her embrace of emptiness and her turning toward her authentic experience of this extraordinarily stressful situation that she was able to take the next step with an open, compassionate heart. This doesn't mean that her path ahead wouldn't be difficult, even often quite painful, but it does mean that a layer of suffering had been removed.

The Antidote to More-ing: Enoughing

Another facet of the jewel of emptiness that empowers us to abandon our attachment to more-ness is close kin to gratitude, but it's easiest to think of as *enoughness*. Enoughness is the tonic that remedies the endless pursuit of ultimately unfulfilling ideals.

I'm not advocating asceticism or rejecting material comfort. Those are just other forms of attachment. The Buddha dabbled in deprivation on his journey to emptiness, but he only became fully enlightened after taking nourishment and adopting the middle way between extremes. We all deserve to have our basic needs met; perhaps yours are not being met right now. Too often this is due to life circumstances beyond our control, including systemic oppression, trauma, and sheer inexplicable loss. I want to offer bows of love and support to all who live under these conditions.

Enoughness is the realization of the precious opportunity we have to be here at all. It's something that any of us can realize at any time. A guest minister at the Unitarian church I attended in Washington, DC, shared the story of his immigrant ancestors barely surviving their voyage to the US. If they hadn't, he pointed out, he wouldn't be there giving that sermon. If any of our ancestors — not just in the recent past but dating back millennia and beyond to our prehuman progenitors — had not survived to the age of procreation, then we would not be here. Going back further, the primordial cells had to swirl a certain way, the stars had to collide and regenerate in a certain direction, the micro-inflations of the big bang had to be inconceivably precise... *everything* had to be pretty much *exactly* as it was in order for you to be you. I don't know what else to call our being here but a miracle.

With this understanding, just one breath, just one footstep, just one glimmer of the sun through this window behind my laptop is enough. So, so enough. We didn't buy any admission tickets or post any deposits before our birth. This life is given to us for nothing, entirely rent-free. Despite our collective fascination with the possibility of eternal life, no such debt is owed to us.

Fully embracing this, cultivating it with practice, is like greasing our gears as we traverse the path of lessening. It has a way of lightening the demands we've made of ourselves, fading the intensity of the perfectionist goals we have been fed by our cultural dream and have readily consumed. It frees us from traditional ambitions and, unencumbered by those distracting attachments, can unleash truly generative and fulfilling creativity in our work.

The Empty Career

For the first fifteen years of my career as I mored and mored, my income never really changed. At one point, in the cool basement of my friends' DC duplex, I had an all-night "Jerry Maguire moment," furiously scribbling an array of scattered visions that would become an online database of health policy analysis. I spent several stressful months collaborating with coders around the world to construct the thing, weathered its crashing during its launch day and subsequent live demos, and poured innumerable hours and dollars into building out its content over the coming years. How much profit (or fulfillment) did this new venture produce? Zero. I've got plenty more of these stories.

After I gradually embarked on the path of lessening, I loosened my grip on the narrow, strictly financial definition of success, stopped chasing each of my shiny new ideas, empowered my staff, and focused on the most essential aspects of my role in the team I was fortunate to build. With a few mindful breaths, an "all-consultant" meeting in a stale boardroom became a matter of genuine curiosity, an opportunity for creativity. I was still full of attachments, for sure, but moments of awareness of the deeper truths of my work life became more frequent and sustained.

Committing to my morning meditation practice and

grabbing opportunities for reflection in real time made me more audacious in generating new policy ideas and solutions for my clients, more nimble and productive in difficult conversations, and less inhibited by fear in leading a team and growing our impact. I was more comfortable letting my truer self come through, instead of relying on the professionalized veneer that I thought people preferred to see.

I found that each conversation, as it was, was enough; this task was enough; I was enough.

What happened then? How much income did I lose as I embraced this more evenly paced approach to my career? None. My consulting firm shifted into a more mission-driven direction. We began attracting more of the type of work that we found truly fulfilling and inspiring. All the while, I was working less and earning the same amount.

I have been extraordinarily privileged to meet such success; I won't peddle false promises that our work efforts will always yield such rewards, or in equal measure to all people. But I can attest to the clarity and productive energy that arises when we release our stranglehold on the ideal of accrual. If we can recognize the emptiness of the components of our workday and be present with the enoughness of our lives, we can know a freedom that the particulars of our career cannot diminish. We can thrive.

REFLECTION: Acknowledging Your Work

Here again you might take a moment to consider the details of your work experience. Start easy: Just relish the moments and scenarios that you already enjoy. Lean into those — how do they feel? What about them fuels your passion and creativity? Or dig a little deeper and investigate one of the more challenging aspects of your work or career. Can you spot an opening to view it from a different perspective? Look, and look again. Notice what you find. What would it be like to bring an attitude of enoughness here? How would that feel? How might you respond differently?

You can expand the scope of these lessons out into your broader mindset toward your work and career. Life hacks and efficiency strategies aren't the domain of this book and, too often, compiling those can eerily lead us back to where we started on the path of ever-increasing complexity. The way of lessening is not about adding new tactics; it's about distilling our attitude to better recognize the essentials. It's prioritizing, yes, but from a new, more vivid awareness of our deepest values and the beauty that's always present.

The Art of Lessening Work

In addition to finding opportunities for real-time reflection, how can we proactively cultivate the way of lessening so that it's more readily available during our workday and throughout our career? As with other emptiness practices, we can take something that has been handed down to us from ancient times and evolve it to connect with the reality of our life right now.

It starts with inhaling the negative aspects of our awareness and exhaling them with positive intention, what many Buddhists call Tonglen. It can work in a variety of contexts, but I find this structure translates well to professional life, perhaps because, for many of us, the reality of our job's stresses, frustrations, and fears is so readily accessible. This is a tool for contradicting the logic of attachment and the suffering it causes. Rather than avoiding unpleasantness, we invite it in. Rather than clinging to positivity, we feed it back out into the world. Rather than simply being a "power of positive thinking" trick, it trains us to open up to a new way of being.

Here we will adopt the essence of this technique and redirect its power to cultivate a new relationship with our work. Its pattern is like a massage for these discrete aspects of our professional life. It can soften them, relax them, make them more pliable. In this way, it can help us enter into the moments of "kalamata olive awareness" described above. It can help us see through our mind's construction of things so we can realize the unblemished possibilities of their emptiness. It is work done "on the mat" (or in the chair) — time in the gym, if you will, to create more opportunities for clarity and peace during the rest of your day.

MEDITATION: Transformative Breath

Sit comfortably, finding a posture that is relaxed and alert.

Let your body be still. Give your feet permission to connect to the floor. Give your hands permission to rest comfortably in your lap. Give your back permission to lengthen. Give your eyes permission to soften.

Allow yourself a few moments of rest.

Here again you might notice the fact that you are breathing. Perhaps find the location in your body where your breath is most prominent. It may be helpful to let your focus settle on your nose or upper lip.

Feel the cool of the air as it enters. Notice the gentle

breeze on your lip as you exhale. Connect with peace. Occupy your seat.

Now you might imagine a challenging situation at work. Perhaps you are sitting at your desk, staring at a conflict-oriented email on your computer. Perhaps you are wrestling with a machine or other technology. Perhaps you are laboring at a construction site or hustling through a hospital hallway, fearing you can't keep up.

It doesn't have to be a certain kind of situation. Any one will do. It may be helpful if it's fairly recent so that you can recall its details without much difficulty.

Take a moment to fully visualize the situation. Notice the details of color and sound, smell and texture. Observe how you feel in that moment, any tensions that might be arising in your body.

Consider a specific aspect of that situation that is challenging for you. See if you can keep it fairly simple. It may help to say it out loud: "I'm angry at my coworker's gossiping." "I'm anxious about how to write this email back to my client." "I'm tired and have several hours to go." Whatever arises first is fine.

Focus on the thought or emotion you have about the situation, and keep that focus as you inhale fully and deeply through your nose. It may help to name it: "angry," "anxious," "tired." Let the negative feeling fill your chest. Inhale a bit deeper now if you can; fill the small corners and crevices of your lungs with it.

As your inbreath begins to turn to the outbreath, just let that bundle of negative concern release to its opposite. If you were angry, imagine directing a soft smile at the object of your frustration. If you were anxious, let yourself be eager. If you were tired, let yourself experience energy. You might name the positive view of the situation this way: "welcoming," "eager," "energy."

Blow that positive feeling out of your mouth, and don't be afraid to sigh, moan, gasp, or shout. Let it out. Give it to the world. Immerse yourself in it. "Ahhhhhhhhhh!!!!!"

Perhaps inhale and exhale through this aspect of your work situation for several breaths, if you'd like. Really dig into it. Feel its contours, both the negativity of the inhalation and the abundant positivity of the exhalation. Make big spacious hungry breaths out of it. Continue with naming the associated thoughts, if that's helpful.

As with many of our practices, this may feel mechanical at first, or outright false. That's to be expected. We are reversing a lifetime of conditioning and eons of cultural inertia. Have no shame in faking it, if that's all you can do right now.

After a few cycles of this part of the practice, consider a new aspect of this situation if there's another to be found. Perhaps in addition to the anxiety about that email, there's a felt pressure to hurry, to always be hurrying. Maybe in addition to being tired in your labor, you have pain in your legs or back. As you scan this situation, it might help to check in with different senses and see what's there.

After you've located a new challenging aspect of this situation, repeat the cycle above. Breathe in the negative feeling you are experiencing there through your nose; breathe it in fully and deeply; let it completely consume your chest and belly; name the feelings as they enter.

Then, just as you feel yourself about to burst with this

adverse emotional state, reverse it to its positive, sustaining counterpart. The hurrying is now ease; the pain is a refreshing tingle. Let that pleasantness blow out of your mouth, pressing it a bit further to make sure it's fully emptied out of you and into your space in the world.

Continue for however long you need to address the noticeable adverse elements of this challenging work situation. Take your time with each in turn. This is not just about resolving that one instance. This is about training yourself to empty your work. You don't need to "think empty"; the invitation is to trust that repetitively balancing these opposites of positive and negative, while attaching to neither, will help massage these sticking points loose. Then the awareness of emptiness can arise more easily throughout your day.

You can also apply this practice to your career on a broader level. Consider an element of it that you find challenging: perhaps a feeling of underachievement, a stuckness or malaise, a sinking feeling that you've been on the wrong path for a while.

Embed yourself in this obstacle just as you did with the challenging situation above. Scan it for discrete negative elements; intoxicate yourself with that breath; brashly flip the emotion or feeling about it on its head; gush your breath of that new positive attitude out to its last sputtering instant.

Fully absorb; fully cleanse. Fully ebb; fully flow. Repeat. Repeat. Repeat.

Once you have cycled through that work situation or career obstacle, settle back into the simplicity of your breath. Let it ease you back into the place where you are. Don't hesitate to let a small grin fill your lips. Don't resist letting your hands rise, flat-palmed, together. Don't deny any gratitude that might rise for the opportunity you had to be with this important part of your life in this strange new way.

◆

This practice is now yours. Take it with you through your career. Be full and then be empty. Realize the truth of your work. May it fulfill you completely.

Chapter 5

Discovering the True Joy of Play

*Our thought now being no-thought, our dancing and songs
are the voice of the dharma.*
— HAKUIN's *Song of Zazen*

I'm bouncing like a newborn elf. I can't remain inside myself.
— TOM MARSHALL, "Guyute"

"Let's go!" I command as I pace around the kitchen. I've been up for hours now and am starting to roast in the four layers of ski clothes I've put on. The foggy, uncaffeinated look on my wife's face morphs into a stinging glance. My kids, also shaking off the cobwebs of sleep, race to finish their breakfast bowls to preempt any further caustic shouts from their dad.

From the house to the frosty morning drive across town to the ritualistic struggle with our bootstraps, I oscillate between barking orders and suppressing my frustration with a thin veil of silence. My young son tears up as he squeezes his growing feet into last year's boots. My daughter silently hustles toward the lift. My wife is ready to ditch me for a latte.

I'm very determined to have fun. Having the opportunity

for us to ski is a big reason I wanted to move to Colorado, and I am going to make the most of it, darn it. I was just starting to get good — ready to graduate from cruising intermediate blue runs to attacking Volkswagen-size moguls on the blacks — and I planned to make more progress today. There would be *quality time* that would include yelling instructions at my kids and the strenuous use of my quads. Then, after all that effort spent joy-making, I'd be ready to saddle up to the bar for my après collapse into a cocktail. This was, after all, my day off....How did I learn to add all these expectations and demands to my playtime?

Many years earlier, I walked tepidly out to the black varnished grand piano on the dusty stage of my lower school auditorium. Staring steadily at my feet, I bowed to the audience before taking a seat on the leather bench. I put my trembling fingers on the ivory, took a deep swallow, and started to press down. I'd practiced this song hundreds of times, each iteration in service to this one moment at the recital. Everything felt strangely still as the onlookers and I waited to find out if I'd navigate the piece successfully. Every ounce of value in this moment seemed to depend on where I'd place my fingers, at what speed, and with what touch. This is how I experienced playing music as a child.

Music stuck with me, though. I picked up an acoustic guitar in middle school, pursuing the well-worn path of the troubadour in search of female attention. For about two decades, I tinkered with both instruments, which provided some welcome relief from the stresses of life. The instruments remained in the outer orbit of my experience, however. Meanwhile, my love for live improvisational music continued to deepen. While running around the local park, I'd mute the pain and monotony of exercise with fantasies of performing mind-blowing solos in front of adoring fans.

Then I spent a weekend with my closest high school friends in Chicago, a bachelor party for a member of our crew. The centerpiece of the event was a three-day run of shows by our beloved band, Phish, a quirky group of music nerds that built a massive cult following through their relentlessly improvised live performances. Somewhere along the way on that weekend, my relationship to music shifted. As the band's bassist, Mike Gordon, wrote in their newsletter decades earlier, "I learned that being awake can be as flavor-specific as dreaming and that sound and motion can be the key to an unknown ecstasy." I decided to make this experience, the true joy of experiencing music, an integral part of my life.

When I got back home, I started taking guitar lessons from a local music co-op called Swallow Hill. My teacher taught me the fundamentals of music theory, which provide the building blocks for improvisation. Unlike my experience as a child, I found great happiness in exploring the elegant relationship between the notes, the symmetry of scales, and the harmony of chords. Meanwhile, I was improving. After a brief jam session where I mentioned that I had taken piano lessons as I child, a new friend from the Zen Center of Denver invited me to join his Grateful Dead cover band as their keyboardist.

At our first practice together, I felt a love for music growing within me that I had not thought possible. Preoccupation with the precision of each note, anxiety about where it would fall, and regret for the inevitable mistakes had all subsided.

In their place was presence. I was not just playing my instrument; I was listening to the music our band was producing as it unfolded. I was experiencing it as it arose, without judgment. Lessening my attachment to the outcome was the only way I could keep up. Only by relaxing, listening, and embracing wherever my fingers chose to go could I really contribute to the art we were creating together. I was improvising. And it was a lot of fun.

Please don't be misled; I am not going to win any Grammys, my bands (I'm now in a few) aren't going to sell out Carnegie Hall (or the local dive bar), and I'm still a far cry from the "real musicians" I admire who make music for a living. It is just a hobby. And, as we might hope for from any hobby, it brings me incredible joy and fulfillment. It's not a distraction or escape from life; it is my life, interwoven with all its other features. I am a musician and I am a dad. There's really no separation between the two, and each positively reinforces the other.

My reopening to the simple possibilities of fun, discovered along my musical path, seeped into other aspects of my life, including on the slopes. Eventually, I stopped my bitter dash for the first chair on the lift. I eased my focus on my performance as a skier to rekindle the joy of simply cruising down those intermediate slopes, completely comfortable to go at my natural pace, welcoming the exhilaration of each turn. I don't try to teach my kids how to ski anymore (they are much better than me now anyway). I don't have any expectation of how quickly we'll get going in the morning or how long we'll last into the afternoon. Just as important, I no longer have the slightest desire to head to the bar when we're done.

It makes me a little sad to think back to those days when I added so much intensity and pressure to the simple privilege of spending a day with my family on the snow. Then I remember that was, after all, just the path I took. It's the path that brought me here, and I am very grateful for it.

The Joy of Empty Play

Perhaps you can relate to the experience of being attached to your play, which may be doing a hobby, socializing, exercising, or other activity that you pursue with the intention of finding some pleasure and relaxation. All too often we bring to these activities our inclination to judge how well we're doing them, or how others around us are responding. We don't just go for a jog; we feel like we must maintain a certain pace. We don't just want to go to a party; we feel like all our jokes have to land. We don't just play poker; we feel we need to win. Rather than experiencing the delight of play, we become attached to the outcome. When we go down that path, some degree of disappointment, regret, or other dissatisfaction inevitably follows. If we enter into play from a place of separation, lacking, or imperfection, and expect it to fill that void, it will never fulfill us.

What if we could put down our judgments and attachments when we play? What if we reacquainted ourselves with that childlike attitude, appreciating a hobby simply for its own sake? We can still have an intention to shave our running speed or enhance our poker skills, but what if we let ourselves simply enjoy those pursuits rather than contaminating them with our expectations about how quickly we should improve? Maybe, with a bit of not knowing and curiosity, what Shunryu Suzuki calls "beginner's mind," we might be surprised by what we learn when we play. Play can be an excellent teacher if we allow ourselves to be open to our authentic experience of it, unclouded by the layers of judgments and expectations we tend to add.

Then what? Then we're on the running trail, skipping over the stumps and breezing around the turns. We can smile as we notice, yet again, the slow churn of our middle-aged muscles as they hesitantly awaken. We can witness the burn of our breath on a winter afternoon. We can be there when our body-mind gradually tunes in to its running and the effort begins to ease. We can celebrate when we realize we're almost back home, our lungs and muscles now warm and buoyant, letting ourselves accelerate a bit just because we can. Maybe we'll be surprised to discover that we actually enjoyed ourselves.

Whatever the activity is — working, shopping for groceries, or washing the dishes — we can apply a mindset of empty play. Setting aside our attachment to expectations about our performance or the result, we may find gratitude for the simple opportunity to be in that moment, doing what we do, however it unfolds. Putting down our perceived need to be a certain way or accomplish a predetermined goal, we can rediscover joy.

This opportunity is always presenting itself to us; it's always in plain sight. The invitation of each moment is to arrive at it unencumbered and free. By embracing the emptiness of play, we remove any potential separation between ourselves and what we're doing. We give ourselves to it completely. In that place, the concepts of evaluation or error lose their meaning. The only thing left is gratitude for the opportunity to do it.

REFLECTION: How Do You Play?

Pause for a moment here to consider how you approach play in your life. Maybe pull out pen and paper to write down some of your hobbies and other activities that you pursue for fun. Spend a few minutes with this to really investigate all the different ways you play. Take inventory.

Now, looking at these together, pick one that feels prominent to you. Maybe it's something you've prioritized recently or that you did this morning. Now write down the different thoughts and attitudes that arise for you as you consider this activity. As usual, see if you can just let the pen move freely, without filter, as you let your mind wander through the various aspects of your experience with it. Why did you get interested in it? Do you do anything to prepare? What standards do you hold for it — any goals or expectations? How has it been going? What parts have you enjoyed? What parts have been frustrating or disappointing?

There are no right or wrong answers to these questions. The invitation is to acknowledge these elements of the experience as clearly as you can, before judgments arise. Be honest with yourself. Perhaps this hobby brings you unbridled joy. More likely, your experience of it is mixed with some degree of reservation, resistance, or incompleteness. This form of play is probably not quite what you think it should be.

The Emptiness of Play

To explore the emptiness of play, I'm going to use an experience that is close to home for me: playing the keyboard at my band's recent performance. You are invited to track this process with a recent experience of play that stands out for you; it can be a sports contest, an artistic endeavor, or just roughhousing with your kids on the floor.

So many facets and sensations constitute this experience. For me, starting on the inside and moving out, there are my expectations and planning, excitement and anxiety. Over the past several weeks, I've listened to the songs on the set list for our next gig, charted out the chords, and practiced my parts. I'm bringing all that with me to this experience.

There's also the equipment I lugged onto the stage with me. There are two keyboards resting on a metal stand, a microphone dangling in front of my face, about a dozen wires connecting everything to each other, pedals to create different sound effects, and amplifiers. All these items are interwoven with those streaming from the five spots on the stage occupied by each member of the band. Each element steers toward a mixing board managed by the sound person and then onward to the speakers facing the crowd. The next time you go see a band, take a good look at the floor of the stage. It's probably chaos.

Moving further outward, there are my bandmates themselves, each bringing their own history and mindset to this moment, feeding their experiences and intentions into each note they play. There is the crowd responding to the sounds we create, some listening quietly in the back of the room, others chatting at the bar, others boogying on the dance floor. As I survey the room, I'm collecting the energy I perceive from each of these camps, catching an eye or two, then staring back down at my fingers as they press the black and white keys on the keyboards in front of me.

Then there is the sound, this mixture of instruments and vocals and effects we're creating. There's each pitch and tone delivered by the ten or so different wired inputs merging to form our song in that moment. The next wave of sound hits, and then the next. Here each of us is, contributing to what arises and, simultaneously, reacting to it. A missed note pops up there, a detour from the chorus here, a solo yielding to another after that, then a glance from our leader to indicate a return to the verse.

Of all these elements, which one makes this a "band performance"? We can look underneath the surface of each individual component — my keyboard, the strobe light, the sound of this one note — to recognize its emptiness, its effervescent impermanence, its absence of any core feature that defines it as what it is. Taking them all together, the emptiness of this experience is undeniable. Who dares to track the streams of history and causation and effort and indecision that swirl to produce this instant of music? How can we possibly claim to know where it came from or be so bold as to define precisely what it is?

Try as we might, there's nothing here for us to attach to. It's all gliding right through us. If we're attuned to it, we just let it flow as it will, and play on.

Playing with Equanimity

The theme of play feels like a perfect fit for exploring the Buddhist principle of equanimity. Cultivating equanimity can help us remember the simple presence that each moment offers, particularly the things we do for fun. Adopting this mindset — a spirit of playfulness — can help us generate a more authentic response to life as it arises, whatever the circumstances may be.

Equanimity can be thought of as the state of being that arises when we set aside attachments. It is a mindset of not knowing, not expecting, and therefore not judging. It's a clean slate that lets the next moment write its truth onto it without any interference. It pairs nicely with curiosity, both inspiring it and drawing inspiration from it. With equanimity, we can find ourselves excited to discover what the next moment will bring. When our expectations are set aside, the road to dissatisfaction begins to fade. Any possible outcome can be an unblemished surprise.

Like its cousin, emptiness, equanimity can be misconstrued as apathy or indifference. We might believe that it is about ignoring the feelings that naturally arise within us as we pursue an activity, closing ourselves off to whatever version of joy or sorrow it might bring. You may have an inkling by now, though, that the opposite is the case. Equanimity is the posture that allows us to experience moments for exactly what they are. We don't turn away from any of it.

We can even bring the spirit of equanimity to perceived misfortune. The ancient Chinese parable of an old man and his son losing their horse provides an excellent example of this. In brief, their horse runs off one day into enemy territory. The local townspeople express sympathy for this misfortune, saying, "What bad luck!" The father responds, "Maybe so, maybe not. We'll see."

Later, the horse returns along with seven more wild horses. Everyone congratulates them for this good luck. The father responds, "Maybe so, maybe not. We'll see." The next day, the man's son takes one of the new horses out to train it and it throws him off, breaking his leg. As you may expect, the locals bemoan this bad luck, but yet again the old man responds with equanimity, "Maybe so, maybe not. We'll see."

Soon their country is at war with the enemies nearby and there's a draft. Because of his injuries, the son is exempted from serving and allowed to remain in the safety of his home. Everyone celebrates this as an excellent stroke of good luck, but again the old man's mind is clear, repeating, "Maybe so, maybe not. We'll see."

You can continue telling the story from here. The truth is, we don't know what the implications of each moment are or the consequences of it that will follow. The causes and conditions of every event are too numerous to imagine and so too its manifold outcomes. Put more simply, we can never know for sure where each new moment will lead. The lesson of equanimity is to stop pretending that we do.

I am not intimating here that we ought to celebrate a cancer diagnosis or the passing of a loved one, or the ongoing oppression and injustice that so many around the world face. This practice is never about bypassing authentic life experience. What the spirit of equanimity can show us, however, is that maintaining an open mind and heart can help us acknowledge the plain truth of our lives, which empowers us to respond to it with our most authentic intentions. There is no obligation imposed on us to react to our life circumstances in a certain way. We are free.

Facing Our Discomfort

A consistent feature of play, as with our broader lives, is discomfort. We may be anxious about an upcoming performance or regretting the mistakes we made that caused us to lose a game. We may yet again be confronting our insecurity and self-doubt as we wade into learning a new instrument or art form. We might find ourselves getting angry at a teammate or even our own child who we determine is not playing the best way they should. More concretely, we might sprain our wrists learning to snowboard or have back spasms when we pick up tennis in our forties.

These scenarios demonstrate how play can be a helpful teacher, particularly when difficulties arise. Just as I was writing this chapter, a friend sent me an article from *Scientific American* titled "Learning to Accept Discomfort Could Help You Thrive." The piece describes several recent scientific studies that document the "benefits in turning toward discomfort or upsetting emotions" without judging them. For example, a 2022 study of more than two thousand people showed that pushing ourselves into uncomfortable situations, like an improv class, can yield substantial gains in our well-being.

A more recent study "found that people who can face negative emotions like sadness and anger in a neutral way are more satisfied, are less anxious and have fewer symptoms of depression" than those who judge their adverse emotions more severely. The authors of the article defined the mindsets tested in these studies as equanimity. They conducted their own inquiry of 153 adults who were offered mindfulness meditation training; some received a specific equanimity-based component to their training and others did not.

After just fourteen days, those in the former group had lower biologically produced stress responses, blood pressure, and stress hormone levels. In other words, equanimity, particularly when applied to our challenges, is good for us.

When I was teaching about equanimity in a recent class, a student objected sharply to these ideas, recounting a story where a physician appeared to be callous about the fate of a patient who had died in their care. That, he said, was equanimity, which has no place in important life-or-death situations like this. Another class participant, a physician, responded that it is exactly in such situations, where we might find ourselves most attached to the outcome and most distraught over a mistake, that equanimity is so direly necessary. She was an ob-gyn and described a situation in which a birth was not proceeding as planned. It's exactly at that moment, she said, that the doctor and other caregivers need to practice equanimity: to acknowledge what was happening, to inquire into it without letting their judgments and reactivity take hold (embodied, as she put it, by staying calm), and to then take the most helpful, caring next step.

Equanimity is the embodiment of wisdom and compassion and a skillful means for accomplishing both in our lives.

The Equanimity of a Tree

Julia Butterfly Hill is an environmental activist who lived in a California redwood tree for 738 days to protest deforestation by a lumber company that intended to cut it down. In an interview after the event, she said that the first three months were the most difficult. Broken physically, mentally, and spiritually, she recognized that she still harbored deep-seated attachments to things like comfort, fear, frustration, and sadness.

Then a storm came, lasting eighteen hours. The winds howled at 60 to 70 miles an hour, with gusts even stronger. Hail pummeled her and rain soaked her as she was tossed among the branches. With her teeth, muscles, and eyeballs clenched, she believed the only way she could survive was to hold herself as tightly as possible.

At the nadir of her despair, a voice inside her pointed to the nearby trees. Looking up, she saw them bending and swaying, their branches dancing in the wind. They weren't just surviving, they were playing. She realized that the trees that are stiff and unyielding are the ones that break. The ones that survive storms like this are the ones able to flow with the wind. Following their lead, she still held on to her place, but her whole body relaxed and her mind was at ease.

She later reflected, "I had to have my attachments broken because attachments make us solid.... You can't be a true vessel if you're attached. You have to be emptied out first." Finding her peace within the storm, she was able to stay in the tree for almost another two years.

Emptying out our attachments allows us to enter a state of equanimity. Equanimity doesn't mean we let our life events topple us. Hill didn't let go of the tree and plummet to the depths below. It means we face obstacles directly, acknowledging their truth so we can bend and sway with them, and then allow them to pass through. All the while, we honor our truest nature, which is not separate from that of a tree.

Hill now knew that she would overcome those who opposed her efforts. Once she had abandoned her attachments, even to her own life, she knew her opponents were powerless to harm her. As she said, "You're not taking my love; you're not taking my exuberance; you're not taking my zest for life." That redwood tree still stands today.

The Art of Lessening Play

We have spent a lifetime and, culturally, millennia adding *more* to our play. We have muddied our experience with preconceived expectations, rigid goals, and punitive methods. We've taken something intended to provide simple joy and polluted it with judgment, zero-sum mental scorekeeping, and the inevitable frustration that follows. So how do we start to reverse these impulses and bring a new heartfulness and freedom to our play?

Here are some tips. Rather than using a hierarchical process, you are invited to explore each of them as they speak to you. We're now about halfway through this book, so you may find you have some extra superpowers to draw on; some of these are referenced below. Fortunately, you may see that they are mutually reinforcing. Practicing one promotes receptivity to the others. So experiment and see what you discover. Play.

1. **Remember your intentions.** Why are you engaging in this activity in the first place? Did you set aside time to play with your child, practice soccer, or watch a concert? Aside from your expectations of the result, how did you hope to be while engaging with this endeavor? How do you choose to experience it?

2. **Embrace your freedom.** Whether you arrived with a plan or are following specific instructions (like

a recipe or musical score), perhaps recognize that, with each new moment, you are choosing where your next step will lead. While following musical notes on a sheet, you are deciding on a rhythm and tone, the strength of your strike on the instrument, or the volume and acceleration of your breath as you sing. Even as you are choosing to abide by certain boundaries, you are still free in each moment. We are always improvising. Relish it.

3. **Recognize impermanence.** This activity has a beginning, a middle, and an end. Also, in each passing moment, it is born anew. This is true for your "performance" of the activity as well. Slower and lethargic now, you may find you are quicker and energetic later. Confused and stalled in deciding the next chess move, you may soon find you are in a flow state where the best maneuver is obvious. The target feels like it's three meters wide right now, and later it may be a pinhole. Your experience of play is always ebbing and flowing, never stagnant. See if you can acknowledge and appreciate that, whichever way it is trending at the moment.

4. **Explore the emptiness of "mistakes."** The famous keyboardist Herbie Hancock tells a wonderful story of performing the jazz hit "So What" with Miles Davis and other acclaimed musicians. Everything was going fine, with Davis ripping one of his brilliant solos. Then Hancock "hit the wrong chord," as he tells it. Immediately, he grimaced and face-palmed,

embarrassed and frozen by his mistake. Davis too briefly stopped playing his trumpet. Then, instants later, Davis started again, this time altering his solo to harmonize with the chord Hancock had struck. "He made my chord right," Hancock says. "He didn't hear it as a mistake. He thought it was his responsibility to find something that fit." We define our mistakes in our minds and, ultimately, that is their only abode. They don't exist anywhere else. So one person's mistake is another's opportunity to carve a fresh, beautiful path, a springboard into an unimagined new moment.

5. **"Dance like no one's watching."** Each of us is probably very well acquainted with the fear and awkwardness we felt as we crept out onto the dance floor at that middle school party. Even now, how many of us scan our surroundings at a concert and subconsciously calculate the right threshold for our movements: Maybe just a gentle head bob fits here, or maybe I can sway a bit side to side. Maybe we adjust ourselves depending on which friends we are with and our understanding of their attitudes. (They are probably doing the same.) See just how limiting our self-consciousness and "other-consciousness" can be? Then perhaps we've had some moments when most of these ideas fell away and we danced our asses off. Maybe we were alone in our kitchen, or perhaps the music was too good to resist and we just let it all go. Truly letting go of our self-consciousness feels so impractical, and our awareness of that has made it a cliché. Just imagine,

though, what your life would be like if you lived this way more often. What would you do? How would it feel? How much fun would you have?

6. **Soften attachments.** In play, as with the rest of our lives, we enter into it with a set of expectations, preconceptions, goals, and judgments. As we have practiced, rather than ignoring or suppressing these, take a good look at them. See how they arise in your mind. To rebalance those deeply ingrained habit patterns, try applying some skepticism. What if they weren't true? What would your experience be like if you didn't believe them? Perhaps these beliefs we once thought were indelible will start to fade a bit. Their centripetal force on us can weaken, and we may find ourselves freer to navigate them as we please.

7. **Be curious.** Remember when you got a new game or toy as a child, or went to a new park? Sure, you likely had some giddy expectations, but part of the excitement probably was that you really didn't know what it would be like. We never actually know what the next moment holds for us. By embracing this place of not knowing, we can be more open to whatever arises. We can recognize that we are creating and discovering new experiences rather than making or earning them. We get to be present for what comes next and discover what it will bring.

8. **Embody play.** What does play feel like in your body? Rigid and clenched or relaxed and soft? When I played baseball, it took me a while to understand

that squeezing the bat and flexing my muscles was the wrong way to swing. "Loose is quick," my coach would say, and quick was power. Loose and relaxed also allows for adjustments, enabling us to deliver responses that are truer to our intentions, whether that be hitting a baseball or connecting with our partner.

9. **Breathe.** Always breathe. Always. Steph Curry, considered the greatest shooter in basketball history, breathes when he releases his three-point shot. Chess players breathe to think; runners breathe for fuel; Xbox gamers breathe for focus. Losing my center at the keyboard, my shoulders tightening and my stomach clenched, I remember that the quickest route to relaxation is breath. Remember it. Practice it. Enjoy it.

10. **Practice equanimity with "success."** A lot of the focus on equanimity comes when we think we need it most: when things are difficult, challenging, frustrating, or disappointing. These are the times when we might remember we read something about equanimity and wonder why it is now so hard to conjure. By applying equanimity to the "good" times, we can build that muscle so it's more readily accessible when things go south. After we score the goal, nail the concerto, or are laughing hysterically with our child on the basement floor, we can apply all the same tools listed above. Of course we allow ourselves to enjoy that moment and embrace it fully, and at the same time we can breathe and recognize

it is fleeting and empty. As always, being unattached to what's happening doesn't mean we're neglecting it, not at all. On the contrary, it means we're releasing ourselves into it even more deeply to truly relish every facet of its profound truth.

By now you may have noticed that these practices need not be limited to the time you designate for play. The art of lessening play is the art of lessening your life: recognizing emptiness and cultivating your practice of its many helpful facets. As we soften our attachments and embrace a mindset of equanimity, our life becomes an unmarked field for improvisation and joy.

REFLECTION: Return to Your Play

Perhaps recall the object of play that you settled on during the pause earlier in this chapter. Take a fresh look at it. Consider exploring how some of the tools presented here might apply to that specific hobby or activity. Start easy: The next time you pursue it, just pick one of the items above and see what it's like to apply it to your endeavor. As always, stay open. Maybe it fits naturally and you immediately recognize some benefits. Just as likely, it feels awkward and unfamiliar and you find yourself resisting the potential changes. Both scenarios are equally acceptable and, ultimately, beneficial. Either way, you are inviting an opportunity to experience your play in a new way and discovering fresh aspects of it and yourself.

In addition to applying elements of the art of lessening to our activities, we can also engage with meditation practices that soften our habit energies and open ourselves to experiencing what arises in a different way. I offer the following mindfulness practice to help you expand your capacity for wholehearted play.

MEDITATION: Celebrating Your Senses

Welcome to the open heart of play. You are invited into this gentle place for your body and mind to rest. However you choose to sit, see if you can lengthen your back a bit more, lifting your head gently and letting your eyes and face soften. Let yourself be comfortable. You are at home.

Navigate your way to your breath. It's already rising and falling on its own. All you need to do is notice. Experience your breath however it is flowing through your body: in the nose or mouth, the throat, the chest, or the belly. Just tune in to your experience of your breath, and let that ease you into a spirit of openness to what is here for you right now.

Take a quick pause to peer into your mind. Perhaps it is feeling busy right now, with lots of thoughts and perceptions hustling through. Or maybe it's a still moment; the waves on the lake have eased and the surface is placid. Either way, just notice your state of mind. There it is.

Returning to your body, we're now going to celebrate the full breadth of our experience through our five senses, these doors of our perception. We're going to cleanse them together.

Let's begin by tuning in to the sensation of touch that's arising for you now. Maybe you feel your feet on the floor, the brush of your clothing, or the warmth or cool of the air in the room. Just pause for a moment here to find out what you feel.

You might notice if those sensations strike you as pleasant or unpleasant. No matter what they are, just let yourself feel them, perhaps with a bit of openness and curiosity. Rest here in your touch for a moment.

Now turn to your sense of smell. Breathing in and out of your nose, is a scent arising? Sometimes, the scent we experience is neutral to us, especially if we are at home. In a more unusual place, scents often become more prominent. Again, either way, just notice the experience of the air wafting in and out of your nose. If there's no apparent smell, explore that a bit further. What does neutral smell like? What is it like to experience the absence of smell?

Then you might turn to the sensations inside your mouth. Let yourself take a swallow. Try to experience your tongue from the inside out and wonder: What does this moment taste like? Maybe it tastes like a sip of coffee you had before you started. Maybe you just had a meal or brushed your teeth, and the remnants of those flavors are present for you. Here too the answer may be "neutral" or "no taste." Whatever it is, that's fine. Pause for a moment to consider the contours and finer aspects of your experience of taste a little longer.

Next notice your eyes. Are they wide, dim, or closed? Is your field of vision clear, blurry, or dark? Whatever the position of your eyelids, perhaps begin to inventory the shapes and shades that you see right now. Usually, our experience of sight is so rich that trying to acknowledge it can feel overwhelming. Just pick one aspect of your sight at this moment — an object, a color, a glow — and let your attention settle there. What does it feel like to observe this thing? What thoughts does it prompt for you? You can give that your focus for a moment and then perhaps move on to just one more facet of your sight and let your attention rest there for a while.

In the last step, consider what you are hearing right now. As we tune in, we may find that what we once considered silence is in fact filled with numerous subtle sounds. Let yourself be surprised by what you find here. Maybe let the temptation to go out and grab the sounds rest. Let them come to you; they will make their way on their own. What is the shape of these sounds? What images do they evoke in your mind? Allow yourself the space to experience them fully, sharpening your awareness of these vibrations passing through you. Be with them for a while.

In the remaining moments, perhaps expand and relax your awareness to the entirety of your sense experience right now. Let the analysis rest. You're just breathing and sensing, sensing and breathing.

Now you are just sitting and aware, open and unblemished. With your expectations and judgments fading, allow yourself to be surprised by what arises next, knocking at your door, bearing its unique message.

This is the practice of awakening: embracing our freedom to greet the next moment with an open heart.

✦

Through our sense perceptions, we can witness the underlying emptiness of every facet of our lives. Softening our attachments and judgments, we can welcome whatever arises with an attitude of openness and curiosity. With this spirit of equanimity and a posture of play, we can ripen ourselves for the authentic and abiding experience of joy.

Chapter 6

Coming Forth in Compassion

Strangers passing in the street,
by chance two separate glances meet.
And I am you and what I see is me.
— PINK FLOYD, "Echoes"

The very nature of our heart is to care.
— TARA BRACH, *Radical Acceptance*

My wife and kids start to pick up their pace, scurrying ahead on the sidewalk and across the street at the next light. My seven-year-old son looks back anxiously as my voice continues to escalate. Oblivious to the passing traffic and curious onlookers, I'm starting to scream. Unconsciously waving my hands to emphasize my frustration, I'm a ball of fury.

We've just begun a yearlong trip overseas, and I'm concerned about how our electric car's battery will fare while sitting uncharged for so long. I was on the phone with the customer support line, trying to purchase a new plug that would fit the outlet at our friend's house where our car was being stored. Suffice it to say, this was not a life-or-death situation.

On the phone with me were my anxieties about the trip, my shame about the attention I was gathering on myself, and the beers I had kicked back at lunch. The result was a merciless diatribe at the young person on the other end of the line, at a call center back in the States, who was steadfastly attempting to maintain their focus and dignity in the face of my tantrum. As my voice became hoarse, their motivation and mine waned, and the call ended, abruptly and unresolved.

A few years later, during summer 2020, a local nonprofit with which I was actively involved was struggling to acknowledge and respond to the reckoning with the racism that was unfolding (still) after the murder of George Floyd. Some members of the predominantly white group were participating in protests and signing up for classes to better understand their role in the still-devastating, pervasive oppression and persecution of Black Americans and other people of color in our country. Others, for whatever their reasons, were not.

As this was unfolding, one of the leaders of the organization began sending out emails to the group that many of us considered racist. Responses ranged from determined, if muted, outrage to utter nonchalance. Swimming in these currents, I considered it my responsibility to address these issues as forcefully as I could. I wanted to speak my truth to the situation and reshape it to my standards. I sought dialogue with the leader who had sent the emails and the process concluded with his departure from the organization.

I fired off my own emails to an array of other group members and, as the weeks passed, my tone became increasingly acrid. I was more and more convinced of the virtue of my approach and of the ignorance of theirs. As my temperature boiled, I submitted a letter to the board that announced my resignation and separation from the organization, aggressively criticizing the unnamed majority that I believed was so woefully off base. Then I was gone, severed from the organization and people that, if flawed, I still cared for deeply.

What do these two anecdotes have in common? In the first, it's abundantly clear to me that I was wrong to chastise the customer service representative over such a trivial issue. I let my fears and anxieties take the driver's seat, and I lost my temper. In the latter, I think the correct course to have taken is far less clear. My motivations may have been justified even if my execution of those intentions was imperfect.

What they have in common is that, in both cases, I had fallen into othering the people around me. Rather than seeing them as themselves, I added my own expectations and judgments to the relationships. It is a mode of more-ing our relationships, which only creates distance. Seeing veneers we impose on people as the people themselves is the initiation of dehumanization, the gateway to contempt. When we adopt the illusion of separation from others, we may find we add a layer of suspicion to everyone we encounter — the clerk at the checkout counter, the old friend, the colleague, or the teammate. If we feel separate, we feel alone, and in this place of scarcity, everyone becomes a potential threat. We live on the brink of insecurity and hostility, depriving ourselves of the inherent peace and fulfillment that is our true domicile.

For me, this is no minor matter. It is not just about awkwardness or disappointment in our relationships. Once we step into the breach of separation and lose sight of our inherent, underlying unity, we have begun to other. While this may lead to only minor, even trivial discord in some of our interactions, it is the same seed of separation and dehumanization that precipitates injustice, conflict, and unspeakable horror. We can simply look at our world now or into the not-too-distant past to see stark examples of humans disregarding the humanity of others. There is a vast difference of degree, to be sure, but I believe that the seeds of dehumanization and othering that we harbor for other drivers on the highway are the same seeds that grew to become the darkest chapters in human history. These are the stakes of our compassionate practice.

Fortunately, there is another path. If we can soften our attachment to our ideas of how our relationships should be, we clarify our view of the unifying commonality of our experience as human beings and the absence of any coherent, identifiable boundaries between us. In our heart of hearts and truth of truths, whatever our circumstances and perspectives may be, we are fundamentally indistinct from one another, however pervasive and intransigent the illusion of separateness may be. We empower ourselves to see this when we lessen our attachment to others as *other*.

Recognizing this doesn't mean I can't persevere in purchasing the part I need for my car. It definitely does not mean I cannot mobilize for the cause of racial justice, in the streets, in the organizations with which I'm involved, and in my own heart-mind. In fact, for me, this core realization is the primary motivation for me to do just that. What changes is how I am in relationship with others. We call it compassion.

Living in Compassion

We are all well acquainted with the emblems of othering. Approaching relationships that way, we are prone to conflict and lacking resolution. What does it feel like to come forth in the awareness of emptiness, softening our attachment to our closely held ideas about others, lessening the clutter of our perspective to see and respond to them more clearly? In such a moment, bitterness feels like a poison. Compassion arises as the norm. Let's compare these two mindsets side by side:

OTHERING	EMPTYING
Suspicion	Trust
Fear	Safety
Caution	Courage
Anger	Kindness
Confusion	Clarity
Resentment	Forgiveness
Conflict	Collaboration
Hostility	Peace
Discord	Resolution
Stagnation	Progress
Oppression	Justice

This table may serve as a reminder of how familiar we are with each path. How many times have we found ourselves caught on the left-hand column? Then, perhaps too briefly, we have experienced the truth of the right-hand side. We have had a task to do, a disagreement to resolve, or a cause to support, and we did so with a peaceful heart, embodying the outcome that we sought. We may also have discovered that the latter approach tends to be much more successful in fostering the outcome we seek.

This is the reason I chose the fraught issue of racism as one of the anecdotes to introduce this chapter. Of all the manifestations of separateness and othering, racism is among the most poisonous, certainly for the oppressed but also for the oppressor. What can and should I do, as a white person, to combat this tide in my day-to-day interactions and in my engagement with the community around me? Whatever answer I discover, I know that if I pursue justice from a platform of fear and hostility, viewing those who practice either indifference or outright persecution as fundamentally separate from me, then I am only worsening the core problem. I'm hardening the separation that is the lifeblood of hatred.

This path I am describing is the opposite of indifference or passivity. As we will explore in more detail later in this chapter, it is a path of emptying our rigid preconceptions, acknowledging the truth of what is before us, and taking action to address it. This applies to both our relationships with the people we encounter and our endeavors to shape a more just and peaceful world.

This chapter pairs naturally with the next one, which is focused on loving-kindness in our more personal relationships. It may be helpful to think of exploring compassion as extending to our involvement in the world, in all its many directions. In the next chapter, we click the microscope to focus more on how we interact with those closest to us, the ones we love. For both, however, the same underlying truth of emptiness and nonseparation can govern, yielding natural fruits of harmony, equity, and joy.

REFLECTION: Acknowledging Our Othering

Pause here to locate a moment when you were deep in the well of separation. Who is your customer service representative; in what situation were you fully absorbed with the spirit of othering, perhaps venting some hostility in a way that you quickly came to regret?

Please be patient as you explore this situation. Consider the context in which you found yourself, perhaps the frame of mind you carried into it. Some stress was likely arising from uncertainty or fear about the outcome. What details of the challenge needed to be resolved? Who were the people you were interacting with? How did you think about them at the time? Who was your ally, and who was your opponent? How did you think about them? Describe those people as you saw them then. I invite you to write down all these streams of thought. Take special note of the contours of how you imagine yourself in that situation relative to those around you.

After five to ten minutes of this, pause to observe and reflect on how the situation arose. Preconditions, evolving circumstances, and relationships all created this situation. If we can begin to open ourselves to acknowledging them fully, we may train ourselves to see the smoke before the fire catches hold. In common parlance today, we might say we are looking for triggers, though if we are looking for them only externally, our search will be incomplete. As we look inward, we are not seeking to resolve or reverse these behaviors right now. The first step we are taking is deepening our awareness of them.

Compassion for the Empty Other

In Buddhism compassion is at the heart of the bodhisattva ideal, dedicating one's life to the well-being and liberation of others. Thus the first Bodhisattva Vow frequently recited by practitioners states, "The many beings are numberless, I vow to liberate them." This "vow" of compassion, however, is not something outside us that we aspire to. It is an underlying truth that we awaken to as an inherent feature, perhaps the core feature, of our daily existence.

All beings co-arise with us, from the ancient past to the infinite future, each unique one always in a constant state of change, eternally becoming. Each also lacks an inherent identity — any core feature that makes it the thing we treat it as. In other words, the many beings are numberless because they are infinite and also because they are empty — that is, unnumberable.

As we have explored, suffering arises when we lose sight of this underlying truth. We attach to the things and people around us as fixed and separate. As their impermanence and lack of selfhood resurface, when we rediscover that there is in fact nothing to attach to, our expectations are failed and we suffer. So it is for all beings. This is why the term *compassion* — or *co-suffering* — is the closest word we have to our relationship to the world. We are fellow travelers in an endless cycle of false attachments.

Our vow to liberate ourselves and all beings, then, is

simply abandonment of this cycle. The path of emptiness lights the way, serving as a guide to abundant love. It unfolds when we recognize the inherent emptiness of ourselves and those around us. There are no barriers to divide us; we are unified at our roots. Our qualities, quirks, and even conflicts can be acknowledged as unique, temporary presentations of the underlying substrate from which we all arise. When we honor this, we can be in relationships governed by compassion.

Here again we can see the two aspects of reality converge: the relative and the absolute. When we talk about abandonment, we do not mean we are ignoring the manifold features of our world, its distinctions, wonders, or even its horrors. Abandonment is the softening and eventual release of our attachments to these things as fixed and separate. In her book *The Way of Tenderness*, Zenju Earthlyn Manuel describes this as multiplicity in oneness. "Multiplicity in oneness," she writes, "does not mean that our preferences, opinions, likes, dislikes, or even hate cease to be present. Everything is here." Giving those distinctions "an 'inner bow' allows us to experience the whole landscape of oneness."

Our differences are not to be ignored. That is not compassion. They are to be honored as the gateway to recognizing our underlying unity. This is, after all, how we encounter each other, in our uniqueness. There is no other way. Then, with our mindful awareness and open heart, right alongside our differences, we can observe the inherent wholeness that we share. How do we treat each other then? How do we set out on our path to promote peace and justice in our world?

REFLECTION: How Do You Want to Be?

Let's come back to you. Earlier I invited you to fully acknowledge and explore a situation in which you felt separate from others, when the natural state of compassion felt cloudy and distant. Now consider: How do you want to be in the world? What is your intention for your relationships with others — those near and far, similar and different?

Please reflect for a moment, perhaps writing, about how you visualize your best self coming forth. What does that look like? How does your body feel? What is your tone of voice? As you explore these characteristics, see if you can cultivate them right now, as you sit here. It may help to recall an experience when you felt these intentions were honored. Breathe it in and let it fill you. Now take another step.

The Art of Lessening Our Relationships

We can use a variety of techniques to soften our attachments to the ideas of self and other and rediscover the fundamental state of compassion that rests within us and all beings. As with so many such processes, an important first step is to tune in to ourselves. "We cannot fill from an empty cup," says a Buddhist proverb, and we have likely observed this truth in our own lives. When we are weary, discouraged, exhausted, or filled with self-doubt, our capacity and availability for compassionate action can feel constrained.

Consistent with the mindfulness tools we are acquiring along this path, it can be vital to check in with yourself throughout the day. This can be a simple whisper in your mind: "How do I feel right now?" If you are feeling harried, overwhelmed, melancholy, or frustrated, the first step is to acknowledge that these feelings are arising for you. They are real and they are important. Be with the emotion without judgment as best you can. Then conjure some curiosity about where it might reside in your body: maybe it's something obvious like a headache or sour stomach, or maybe it's something more opaque. Often, the prevailing sensation may be numbness.

Looking deeper still, we might examine the contours of our emotions. This applies to positive feelings as well. We might ask ourselves: "What are the causes and conditions for the state I'm in?" It could be as simple as needing a snack or it could be much more complicated. Your inquiry may take you back to emotionally powerful events, perhaps from your childhood. Watching the story as it unfolds, it can be illuminating to notice the stories you are telling yourself about these incidents, the judgments you have layered onto them. In the spirit of lessening, remember our training around thoughts: it can be helpful to rebalance our instincts by applying some skepticism to the stories we have carried with us for so long. Are we obliged to let them govern us as we sit here now?

Wherever the path leads, be tender with yourself. If the waters get choppy, hold yourself with love, trusting that you are safe in this moment. A physical sentiment like putting your hand on your heart, even whispering "It's okay" to yourself, can be incredibly comforting. This is the path of unfolding the truth of you in the moment. There is nothing more important for you to do. Don't forget to breathe. The breath is your fuel for this journey, which might last just an instant or become a deeply compassionate detour from your busy day.

As we conclude our self-examination, we can acknowledge that compassion has layers. On one level, we can simply observe our pain or discomfort, our sadness or frustration. Beneath those emotions, though, we may see that we have been attached to certain ideas, preconceptions, and expectations that add another layer of suffering. This simple act of witnessing the complex intertwining of pain and suffering is the heart of compassion.

Turning to our relationships with others, the process is a mirror image of the one we just traversed. Whoever the person or group of people may be, from the person passing us on the sidewalk to the members of the political party we disfavor, they are worthy of our compassion. We do not have to agree with them or condone their behavior; we will explore the importance of setting clear boundaries in the next chapter. But to bring forth the spirit of our truest intentions, we might consider the possibility that we can hold some compassion for each and every being.

When we turn our gaze in the other's direction, what do we see? The first step can be very simple. What are their features? What is their expression, the tone of their voice? These manifestations are an important part of them. Looking deeper still, we can know that life experience brought them here to this moment; like us, they have had a complicated journey. We won't know entirely what it was, could never really know, but we can assume it has had ups and downs, bends and curves. Most likely quite a few things didn't work out for them the way they'd hoped. They've also likely seen glimmers of joy and peace somewhere along the way. None of this is about excusing; it is simply an exercise in understanding.

Going deeper still, with a settled mental gaze, we may observe that they live in this world of form — of lines and boundaries, distinctions and judgments — just like we do. Like us, they have attached to their own notions of what this world means, of how it should be, and they have done the best their circumstances will allow to navigate it. All the while, like us, these notions of separation, of self and other and good and bad, have caused them tremendous suffering. The Buddha whispers, "All is suffering," and it echoes every time we look at another face. We may be sworn mortal enemies, but neither of us has managed to fully escape the cycles of attachment. How do we feel about them now? What is our best response to this moment that honors our underlying state of co-suffering?

During the course of our busy lives, mustering this patience and clarity can be quite difficult. We may wake up in the morning, maybe we even meditate a bit, and we set out with an intention to bring this compassionate heart to our relationships with people near and far. Then what happens? That telemarketer rings us again and — poof — it all flies out the window. That's okay. This is our practice. Here are a few techniques for keeping your head above the waterline of compassion as best you can:

- **Think of that person (or yourself) as a newborn baby.** There is a reason we call the youngest among us innocent. We can all imagine this state we once inhab--ited, along with all other living beings, when we were truly blameless. We arrived in the world, opened our eyes, and saw the infinite, unblemished expanse that is apparent before ideas and labels rush in, and we knew somewhere in our bones that we were a part of it. We belonged there. Very soon, though, distinctions made their impressions, we carved out our beliefs about the world, and our circumstances began to shape us. Wherever each of us may be now, we were all once there, in that sacred space, "trailing clouds of glory," as Wordsworth wrote. We all share that. It can be helpful to remember this.

- **Pretend (or acknowledge) you have never met.** This can be particularly helpful for people, often those closest to us, with whom our relationships have become rigid. A related practice is to acknowledge the preconceptions we instinctively start to conjure the first time we see someone. As we approach the checkout counter or watch the car pull ahead (perhaps with certain bumper stickers that trigger certain judgments...), we start to tell ourselves a story about that person in our minds. So whether or not our ideas about a person stem from past experience, it can be an interesting practice to set all that aside for a moment and see how our mindset changes. As we'll explore in the next chapter, nothing that person does is our responsibility, but how we come forth into the relationship is. We can decide whether our perspective is stony or soft, bounded or free. We could say we are pretending to have a clean slate, but in the ever-changing nature of our reality, in fact, that is always the case.

- **See the empty canoe.** The Taoist master Chuang-Tzu offers an allegory we can explore to cultivate compassion. If we are floating down a river and we see a canoe heading directly at ours, it is natural to grow concerned and then perhaps frustrated that someone is being so inconsiderate. We may even begin to tell ourselves a story about that person. What might have caused them to be so reckless, to have such disregard for another person? We might start to get angry at them; maybe we start to shout insults. But then, as the canoe approaches, we find that it is empty. It has just floated into us as a natural consequence of its weight and direction and the current of the river. How do we respond then? We can still paddle out of the way — no need to let the canoe hit us — but hasn't our whole experience of the run-in with the canoe changed?

- **Put your trust in tenderness.** I suspect we all know what it feels like to be in a reactive state. We have sensed ourselves in conflict, frustration, and anger. We have reacted harshly to situations that probably didn't warrant it; we have cast harmful words at others that only served to harden the perceived separation and otherness that divide us. Also, though, we can remember what it feels like to respond to a situation with peace. We know what it feels like to be in accord with our heart center. One of the most obvious examples of this for me are the moments after I've had the opportunity to go on an extended meditation retreat. My mind and body have been still for an extended period. In those situations and the (often, alas, brief) time that follows, I feel incredibly tender. My body is soft, my eyes are soft, my words are soft.

We are told that we have to be "strong" in the world, to have our guard up and be ready to pounce at the slightest offense. But has that posture really served us? Has it brought us the peace and fulfillment we seek? Maybe it has just fueled ongoing cycles of conflict and isolation. We can still have boundaries, we can still protect ourselves, but the most effective and satisfying way to do that may well be to bring our walls down and let it all pass gently through.

Compassion in Action

So far we have considered some attitudes and tools for cultivating compassion for individuals and groups of people with whom we interact. The call of compassion invites us further, though, to extend this aspect of ourselves into the world at large, acknowledging that it too is not separate from us.

There is a danger in misunderstanding that mindfulness practice and Buddhist ideas are only for our own benefit. The goal of this path, we might believe, is simply to feel better, be happier, and enjoy healthier relationships. Those are certainly worthy pursuits, but alone they are wholly incomplete. The time we spend alone, in silence, meditating on a mat is a fundamental, seamless element of our dedication to the liberation and welfare of all beings. We must also take that next step off the mat and put those intentions into action. Identifying where and how we might best apply this effort is not often easy.

In her generous book *You Belong*, Sebene Selassie wades into the complexity of cultivating compassion in a world of pain. "All spiritual traditions," she says, "mention kindness and forgiveness toward all beings," including our adversaries. At the same time, she recognizes that practicing compassion for other individual people may obscure the fact that systems "are used to carry out oppression." She questions the merit of "talking about feeling non-separation from individuals as children are ripped from their families and placed in flighty cages." Selassie wisely does not resolve this tension between cultivating compassion for all beings and combating oppression; I certainly won't do so here. She doesn't try to paint over it with platitudes. The difficulty of existing in this hurting world and locating the inspiration to come forth in love may be the most important and most painful koan of our lives. I encourage us to follow her example into this difficult, uncomfortable terrain, and to be okay with not knowing exactly where to find our balance among these urgent demands.

What we may recognize is that the root of injustice and systems of oppression is the same separation we experience when our lips snarl at the person inching ahead of us at the stoplight, albeit on a dramatically smaller scale. It is that same root misunderstanding that a person or group that we disagree with is divided from us, perhaps inferior to us. Seeing through this illusion "does not mean accepting injustice," as Selassie puts it, and it doesn't need to mean picking a side, but it does mean taking a stand. And our stand can be for connection, compassion, and peace.

I won't lecture oppressed people who face violence every day — explicit and implicit, obvious and subtle — about the virtues of nonviolence. What this lesson holds for me abides in this Taoist proverb:

If there is going to be peace in the world, there must
    be peace in the nation.
If there is going to be peace in the nation, there
    must be peace in the community.
If there is going to be peace in the community, there
    must be peace in the home.
If there is going to be peace in the home, there must
    be peace in the heart.

If we are going to take that vital step out into the world
and lend it the compassionate action that our time and talent
can muster, I believe we must do so while embodying the
outcome we wish to achieve. It's not that the direction of
our effort isn't important; we can cultivate clarity and discernment to identify our next step. How we take that step,
though, is how we impact the world. Do we take it peacefully,
gently, humbly, and with an open heart and mind? Or are
we marching aggressively, head down, eyes closed, and fists
clenched?

This became abundantly clear to me during my work
with the nonprofit described at the beginning of this chapter.
As I told a friend there at the time, "My anger isn't going
to help anyone heal." In that spirit, when my contempt was
saturating my responses to that situation, stepping away was
probably the correct choice for me. I also had to confront
myself this way in running the alcohol-free bar that my wife
and I started. How could I successfully manage a space dedicated to cultivating presence and connection when I was as
stressed, frustrated, and fearful as I had ever been?

Whatever cause we take up, we might carry with us an
understanding that how we *are* in pursuing that objective will

probably be the most important contribution we make to its outcome. If we stride into our volunteering shift with an axe to grind, whether or not we're able to complete a few tasks, have we furthered the mission of the organization, whether it be for advancing justice or combating hunger? No matter how we prefer to see it, isn't our biggest impact in life on those with whom we directly interact? Aren't those the seeds we are planting in whatever our chosen cause may be?

The Art of Peacemaking

There is another teaching along the path of compassionate action that has supported me and that I'd like to pass along to you. As articulated by the Zen master and founder of the Zen Peacemaker Order, Bernie Glassman, we can follow a three-step process for cultivating peace and justice in our world:

1. **Not knowing.** The practice begins with setting aside our preconceived ideas about self and other, right and wrong, even truth and illusion. We cultivate letting these attachments pass through, gifting ourselves the clarity and power of fresh eyes and hearts.

2. **Bearing witness.** Untainted by prior concepts, what do we see when we look out at the world? This means seeing the totality of the situation, not just from the perspective of the victim, for example, but also from that of the perpetrator. Here again the practice is not to condone or pick a side. The call and the challenge is to visualize every facet of the experience for all involved, from the cold, dark cell to the pain inflicted

to the shame, regret, or grief. This can be an incredibly powerful practice. Please bring along your self-compassion as you take these earnest steps. At the heart of bearing witness is the fact that, in every facet of the situation we explore, we see ourselves.

3. **Taking action.** There is no formula for this except to put one foot in front of the other, one word after the last, one hand extended outward. From the foundations of not knowing and bearing witness, what course calls to you? Where do your time and talents align to foster the change in the world that you would like to see? Bring your love for yourself, your compassion for others, and your peace from your meditation mat, and dive in wholeheartedly.

REFLECTION: Compassion in the Face of Injustice

I'd like to invite you back into a moment of reflection. Take up, if you will, a cause or issue that you feel passionate about. We're looking for the type of issue where you may be inclined to believe very fervently that your perspective is absolutely correct. It is wise, compassionate, informed, and necessary. Those who disagree with or oppose you on this, you might also believe, are wrong. They are ignorant, indifferent, or even malicious. You might pause to really hash out all the aspects of your feelings about your role in this "fight" and your perspective of those on the other side.

Now consider, wherever these thoughts and passions are swirling at the moment, a valid and authentic part of your experience, how do you take the best next step forward in pursuit of justice? Is it with a clenched fist, hatred toward those on the other side, and anger and frustration at anything that gets in your way (including your own tactical mistakes)? Is this really the most effective way to make progress, or is there another way? What would it feel like to be just as committed to your cause, to spend just as much time and energy in its favor, while abandoning your preconceived ideas and judgments about where your efforts will lead, what the result will be, and how it will impact your opponents?

I think we can relate to this if we've been in a meeting, like my experiences working on Capitol Hill, where everyone pretty much agrees with the spirit of what must be done. We are all on the same "side." But there are disagreements about the strategy, and the conversation turns vicious and unproductive. Voices are ignored, characters are impugned, and harm is perpetrated. Meanwhile, how's that cause doing? Are these rigidly held opinions and fierce efforts really the most effective way to accomplish the mutual goal? These dynamics take place in contexts large and small all the time. What does the alternative look like? Voices are heard, reactions are eased, collaboration and creativity are allowed to flourish and, more likely, the cause is advanced.

We can cultivate this compassionate approach to action in those quiet moments we allow ourselves for personal meditation practice. I invite you to approach the following guided meditation in that spirit.

MEDITATION: Softening Our Stories

Welcome back to your seat. There is a lot to feel right here. Take a moment, and allow yourself to settle into your space.

It may be helpful to take a few deep, cleansing breaths. You can honor all the thoughts and feelings that are arising for you right now. Breathing, allow them to gently pass through.

Perhaps check in with your body. What is it telling you about your experience? Are there areas of obvious tension? Are there places of ease and comfort? Is there energy or stillness? Just tune in and notice. There's no need to change how you feel.

To further support your settling, you are invited to focus on your breath for the moment. Perhaps notice where the feeling of the breath is most prominent for you. To focus further still, perhaps name the in- and outflow of the breath or count it as it arises and falls.

You are invited to bring to mind a person you encountered recently who generated some difficulty for you, maybe someone you don't know very well. It can be an impolite store clerk, a driver that cut you off, or a customer service agent on the phone. Maybe it is a new colleague or customer. Pause here to select the person you choose to focus on.

Now we begin our inquiry by considering what you know about this person through your senses. What do they look like? If they spoke, how do they sound? How do they come forth to you as they are; what have you observed of them?

Perhaps take a step further into your mind to examine the thoughts and ideas that you have about this person. What might you imagine about where they came from, their past experiences, even what their childhood was like? What might their beliefs be, their values? What judgments arise in your mind about the type of person they are? It's okay to be as honest here as you can, without judging your thoughts. This is the story you believe about that person, and you will keep it to yourself. Take a few moments to explore it thoroughly, just as it is. Stay with your breath, attuned to your body. How does this story feel for you?

Now the invitation is to go back to the starting point of what you know about the person through your direct experience of them, and start writing a different story. It does not need to be a "good" story; it's just helpful if it's different from the one before. Revisit some of the details and change them, slightly or drastically. You can also add some other details that you didn't consider before. Tell a new story to yourself about this person. Take a little while to let it unfold. Again, check in with how this story feels.

We will pause now, and you can repeat this retelling of your story of that person a bit more. As human beings, we do this a lot, so you have permission to engage with this vigorously, without reservation. Continue to breathe. Continue to feel.

Now you can let the storytelling rest. Just pause here in your breath and body as the churning thoughts settle. From this vantage point, look back at the array of stories you told. Consider how they were similar and how they differed.

Now ask yourself: "Which one is true? Which one do I really believe? How sure am I?" There's no rush to answer these questions. Be with them for a while.

Expanding your lens, ask yourself how many stories you've told yourself about the people you've met. How have these stories influenced your response to them? When you interacted with these people, were you reacting to your story or responding from the place inside you that exists before the story is told?

Be gentle and compassionate with yourself. Hold yourself with a light "It's okay" or "I'm okay." Where are all those stories now? What relationship do they have to these people? What power do they have over you?

In the remaining moments, consider your best next step into the relationships around you, those near and far, new and familiar. Locate the response that comes from your heart center — the response that comes from you. You are always free to speak your truth. You are always empowered to confront unfairness, injustice, and harm — perhaps more so now than ever. What does that look like when it comes from a place of compassion, from the bottom of your heart?

This is the practice of liberation — yours and others'. This is the place where your beauty shines brightest and where your actions have the most power.

✦

This is difficult work. Relationships, in all their complexity and nuance, fragility and fear, as well as our engagement with the broader world around us, with all its horrors and tragedy, can feel like the most difficult places to muster the inspiration of emptiness, the setting aside of our attachments, and the embrace of our underlying unity with all (*all*) that is.

Abandoning our judgments and ideas about these things can feel like denying ourselves or retreating on our values. What we might discover with this practice, though, is our authentic self, the one that has space for all these swirling aspects of our experience to flow through. This is our true home, where we are free to honor ourselves and others, in our uniqueness and our unity.

Chapter 7

Being the Love You Are

Metta... is the natural expression of the free mind.
— RUTH KING, *Mindful of Race*

Without love in the dream it will never come true.
— ROBERT HUNTER, "Help on the Way"

The indulgent French sweets were mindlessly strewn across my plate. My wife Christy and I were having dinner by ourselves at the end of a week spent in the idyllic French coastal town of Cap Ferret. The elegant restaurant and its delicate ambience, the whispers of other couples nearby, and the endless dessert buffet all belied the terse conversation we were having. We had spent years planning this year abroad in France, and this trip to the coast was the apotheosis of our expectations and a final pause before the kids would begin school. In so many ways, everything had gone incredibly right. And yet here we were, feeling incredibly wrong.

Preparations for this trip posed many emotionally charged challenges for me. Having previously left Washington, DC, for Denver, I had to navigate reorienting my professional life yet again for this ambitious year abroad. In the process, I left the firm I had been with for five years to form my own independent company just months before we planned to depart. I anxiously approached each of my consulting clients to let them know about the trip and request their forbearance with this unusual maneuver for a Washington-focused policy advisor. Our initial decision to rent out our Denver home gave way to selling it and all the precious memories we had built there with our two children. I had agreed to the plan, and I wanted to go to France and take each of these steps along the way, but they were tremendously stressful. Meanwhile, my drinking habits continued to deepen. Unbeknownst to Christy, I had consumed about a pint of tequila in the afternoon before our dinner.

Meanwhile, Christy's experience of this time before our year abroad played out with its own challenges for her. Our effort to create this magical bonding opportunity for our family was withering the most important bond we had: our marriage. Over the course of several months of abrupt conversations, passive jabs, and snide remarks, we had grown deeply embittered toward each other. Our relationship had become a barely tolerable discourse on logistics, a far cry from the loving union we intended it to be. In brief, we were unhappy, and we blamed each other.

So that night, as we sat in one of the most beautiful places on earth, with a perfectly humidified Atlantic breeze grazing our skin, we decided to divorce.

Fortunately, the seeds of love and care for each other hadn't completely dried up and disappeared. As I silently grieved our decision on the walk home and carried it with me into sleep, Christy mustered the grace to suggest we reconsider, sent in an email late that night. I woke up to her precious peace offering and we embraced, our glazed eyes seeing each other anew. For the first time in a long while, I saw us for what we were: delicate souls, doing our best to live, carrying the weight of all our pain, suffering, and trauma, wanting so badly to love and to be loved. I had seen just how fragile our relationship could be, and I knew that I wanted to do everything I could to mend it.

During the several hours driving home that day, I examined the path our marriage had taken and tried to generate a plan for how to alter its course. I had been to therapy and coaching and was by then very active with my meditation and Zen practices. I called on all those experiences to show me the way forward. I wasn't quite ready, apparently, to see how much alcohol was clouding this and all my relationships. That fog wouldn't lift completely for another few months. Here is what I did conclude that day: The truest expression of my love for my wife was the abandonment of my attachment to her and all the things I expected her to be, the ways I preferred she behave, and — most of all — the ways I wanted her to respond to me. None of those things had anything to do with her or my love for her.

The best version of my love had to do only with my own expression of that love to her: my words and actions, my presence and listening, my openhearted acceptance of her just as she was. This may seem obvious. It is, in a nutshell, what we usually vow to do when we get married. But how deliberately do we practice it? In fact, our practice of love often sharply contrasts with this intuitive understanding.

We pursue it in a way that is deeply attached to the object of our care, believing it is our concern, even our responsibility, to evoke loving responses from them. If our beloved isn't feeling happy, we tend to believe, then neither should we. Implicitly or explicitly, we might believe that their well-being in fact depends on us.

I am very grateful that I got to see the cliff that path leads to just before I fell off it. As difficult as it was, as much as I might have longed to get back those years I had spent increasingly consumed by anger and blame toward my spouse, it was a gift to be able to walk up to that precipice, take a look over the edge, and turn around. It gave me a new understanding of love — one that is still turning toward tenderness, caring, and connection but that is now centered in a very different place: my heart.

Reverent Love

I think we are all familiar with the attached version of love. With it comes expectations of how we and our loved ones should be ("If you loved me, then you would…") and then the ensuing judgment, blame, and shame when none of us meets those expectations. This dynamic arises in unfulfillable expectations of fairness in the division of labor in the household, or futilely trying to adopt identical parenting styles, or assuming that the support our loved one needs in a time of grief mirrors what we need in a similar circumstance. It also includes the disappointment, anger, or frustration we feel when our loved one doesn't "give us what we need": the wrong gesture or gift or the wrong response to ours.

At our wedding over twenty years ago, the Unitarian

minister David Takahashi Morris compared this attached version of love to the traditional marriage metaphor of "tying the knot." When our love is a tied knot, we are holding the other person in place with our demands and expectations while we cling to them so tightly that we are also unable to move. There is no space to freely be ourselves in this kind of relationship and grow over time. Everything is bound up with our ideas of what love should be and locked in place the moment we tie that knot in the wedding ceremony.

Perhaps a better way to think of our love, Takahashi Morris suggested, is as a pair of extended hands, resting flat, palm to palm against each other, gently. This way, the people in love are connected but are also able to move in their respective directions as life unfolds, gliding and dancing freely in tandem. They are present to provide support to each other but also to allow and honor the other to be who they are. As our minister described this, he slid his hands slowly up and down and around to demonstrate what this type of love looks like in motion. There is an elegance to this version of love, a grace, and a rhythm. "And when it comes to rest," he said, stilling his hands in the position we often equate with prayer, what Buddhists call *gassho*, "it takes a form that is familiar to us all."

REFLECTION: How Are You Attached to Love?

I invite you to pause here for a moment of reflection, perhaps taking up your pen and paper. Consider the ways in which you are attached to a particular idea of love. What do you think love should look like? Describe that with as many adjectives as you can. What does love require of you? What does your love expect of others? You might write down certain thoughts, words, or behaviors. What does your idea of love look like in action?

As usual, there are no right or wrong answers here. This is just a moment to notice what love means to you now and has probably meant to you for some time. It has likely served you well in many instances, perhaps not so well in others. That would be typical of the human experience. It certainly is of mine. So, abiding in your compassion, be honest with yourself and let the ideas flow just as they arise for you until you are comfortable you have exhausted them. This is just a practice of acknowledging.

Empty Love

The principles of understanding the emptiness of love are similar to the themes we have explored so far, particularly those relating to compassion. In this chapter we are just fine-tuning those teachings and practices to our more intimate relationships, the ones we share with those closest to us.

We can start by recognizing our traditional notion of ourselves and of all things and of everyone around us as containing a permanent, coherent self and leaves us irreconcilably separate from one another. This perceived separation invariably generates judgments about everything we encounter as serving or disserving, pleasant or unpleasant, attractive or repulsive. We find ourselves pursuing, often craving, those things we deem pleasant, driven primarily by the fear that we will not be successful in obtaining them or that, when we do, we will lose them.

When we live this way, though, we will never and can

never be satisfied, because the things we seek do not have the qualities we ascribe to them. They are, in fact, impermanent and lacking a core, definitive self. We are chasing an illusion and thus always end up empty-handed. That is our suffering.

When it comes to love, this is often a self-fulfilling prophecy. Yongey Mingyur Rinpoche jovially describes how, when we meet someone we are attracted to, we often act like a fool, contrary to our true selves and to our aspirations of achieving love. Our unsteadiness in such circumstances (of which, believe me, I am well aware) stems from the fact that we're operating in a state of subtle aversion: the fear of losing the person we desire. It's a very uncomfortable and unstable place from which to express love.

During a recent class I was teaching, we had a good laugh recalling the scene from the movie *Swingers*, when Mikey tries to resist the temptation to immediately phone a woman he has just met. He ends up calling her almost as soon as he gets home, and then calling back after the voicemail time expires, and then again to apologize for that, and then again to acknowledge that was weird, and then again and again and again. I suspect Mingyur Rinpoche would have a chuckle at that one too.

This is often not too far off from how we act, and it is okay. It's helpful to take a look at ourselves and have a good laugh sometimes. This same spirit of attachment arises throughout the course of our loving relationships too, and on some of these occasions it is not so funny. Believing in our separateness and thus our perpetual imperfection and lacking, we seek others with the expectation that they can fill our void — we expect them to "complete us." This is how we get caught in the trap of always trying to add more to ourselves, to others, and to our love.

The result: We might find ourselves in a full-throated scream at that person we love because they are somehow not living up to these unattainable expectations we have placed on them. Our insecurity has become a tornado, and we are redirecting the whirlwind their way. Or we might end up in deep despair because the object of our care has stopped loving us in return. We might feel ashamed, inadequate, and, again, isolated. We might begin to suspect that we are not capable of love and that neither are others.

And actually, we are right: No one can live up to the perfectionist ideas we have conjured about love when it is built on the foundation of separateness, craving, and attachment. Sadly, so often love is part of a tragic cycle: It begins with affectionate desire and ends with bitter aversion.

Once we start to see that this attitude about love does not actually serve us or those we care about, we might be open to turning toward the emptiness of love as a new path. What if we put down our preconceived ideas about love or how those who love each other should behave? What if we allowed this labyrinth of judgments to fade and we looked anew at the people around us? What if we remembered the underlying truth that each of us is always changing, preciously impermanent, and lacking any essential qualities that divide and distinguish us from one another? Could there be a moment when we pause and realize that we are growing from the same root, the source of all being that, lacking nothing, is always whole, complete, and indivisible? How do we love then?

The Art of Lessening Love

Embracing the way of lessening in our relationships means releasing our images and expectations of who others are and how they should act. Instead, we focus on our own truth and honor it by setting clearer boundaries around our zones of responsibility, meanwhile softening our attachments and dependencies. This integrity with ourselves is how we lessen and thereby realize love; it's the antidote to the more-ing of others that results in harmful codependence and ties the immovable knot. So how do we distill our love so it can manifest authentically, honoring how we are all always changing and also fundamentally united at our root?

Step one, as is so often the case, is to simply and mindfully acknowledge what is. In that spirit, I offer you this definition of love: honoring our mutual freedom to come forth as we are. Love says, "I see you and I accept that you are you, doing what you do." Our true friends, they say, are those who know us well and like us anyway. In those relationships, we are free to do us and they are free to do them. That's love. Mutual respect and kindness ensue.

There are a variety of tools for developing this approach to love in our daily lives. Their common thread is the perhaps paradoxical recognition that setting healthy, mindful boundaries is the practice of freedom and the ultimate expression of love. Rather than cultivating our attachments to ideas of love as binding, fixed, and restrictive, we can open ourselves to genuine love that is unconditional and unbounded — the infinite love offered by our infinite selves in this infinite moment.

In our romantic relationships as with our other compassionate relationships, we can discover that we have space for it all: the joys and sorrows, the connected candlelight dinner, the argument about loading the dishwasher, the arrival of a new, exciting relationship, and the moving on of one whose time has passed. The tactile reality of two humans relating to one another won't go away, but our capacity to be with it a bit more freely and easily can expand as love grows in that spacious abode.

Recognizing Codependency

It may help to begin by fully exploring the suffering that attachment in our loving relationships can cause. For this, I will use the word *codependency*. While it is often understood as a uniquely dysfunctional, even clinically diagnosable condition, I use it here more in the sense of a common aspect of all our relationships. Learning to identify its symptoms and consequences can recenter us on the path of love.

Put simply, codependency arises when we believe that our mental or emotional well-being is predicated on someone else's actions. This reminds me again of Master Adam's simple expression: "Someone says, 'Oh, you look scummy,' and you feel sad." In such an instance, we have given someone else responsibility for our mental state. That is codependence, a deep form of attachment.

This applies in the other direction as well: Codependency is also believing that others' state of mind is to some degree contingent on what we do. For example, we might think it's our responsibility to help our loved one feel happy. We might give them a gift, a kind word, or a favor that we expect will improve their mood and perhaps generate some appreciation. But only that person gets to decide how they respond to our gesture and how it may or may not impact how they feel. Thinking we can control how other people feel is the height of condescension, not love. Our choice of how to be in that moment and their choice are in fact totally independent of one another.

This also brings me back to my experience of depression during college. As I described, I had become so obsessed with what others thought about me and how they treated me that I had lost the ability to experience life from the inside out. I lost touch with my feelings, buffeted by the winds of others' actions. It was paralyzing and agonizing.

My beloved coach and teacher, Cate Gerstberger, shared a more comprehensive definition of codependency with me that I believe captures its spirit poetically, albeit in a way that may be painful to face. She initially received this from her teacher, Rosa Mazone, and she has given me permission to create my own expression of it here for you:

> Codependency is a disconnection from a felt sense of aliveness with a resultant loss of purpose and meaning. As a result, we develop beliefs and behaviors as a way to manage life instead of living life. We become outer focused and seek to control and manage what is outside us in an effort to compensate for what we believe is missing inside. Our insides and our outsides stop matching. A strong need for numbing, self-medicating, and dissociating replace access to our feelings. Relationally, we seek to manage the experiences of others in an effort to find our own sense of safety and worth. At the same time, we turn the responsibility for our own safety and worth over to others.

By projecting onto others this responsibility, we find ourselves constantly frustrated, angry, and full of grievance and a sense of lacking in our relationships.

Codependency is over-reacting to what is outside us and underreacting to what is inside. We turn the volume up or down on anything outside us in life to medicate and fill the hole that has developed inside as a result of unmet needs and self-defeating behaviors.

This is admittedly a grim picture, but perhaps you can see the seeds of this tendency in your own intimate relationships. We may have created ways of adapting to codependency to keep these connections intact even as their other-centered infrastructure persists. If we can tune in to how the mechanisms of codependency are interwoven with our intention to love, though, we can begin to soften their grip and reopen channels of authenticity and mutual respect. That begins with establishing boundaries.

Defining Responsibility Is Freedom

It may seem paradoxical that establishing clear boundaries around our responsibilities creates a framework for more deeply connected, loving relationships. Again, we might consider how our traditional mindset about these relationships has served us. Do we see the ways in which our attachments and expectations are producing unfulfilling results? The closeness we desire so easily gives way to disappointment and anger. When we establish clear boundaries, we lessen those expectations and sever those attachments, which allows us to rediscover what we truly love about the person in the first place.

The first step toward establishing healthy boundaries is truly and wholeheartedly loving ourselves, accepting that we are inherently, unconditionally worthy of abundant love and thereby empowered to share it with others. With this faith in ourselves, we are free to live in accord with our deepest values, characterized by honesty, ease, and equanimity.

What, then, is our responsibility? What aspects of our life are truly within our control that we should embrace as our path to coming forth with love? At the same time, and in contrast, we can define where this responsibility of ours ends and where that belonging to others begins. In doing so, we recognize and cherish their inherent worthiness of love and capacity to express it in their own way. With homage again to my teacher, Cate Gerstberger, for permission to draw from her words, here are some boundaries you might consider:

IT IS MY RESPONSIBILITY TO:	IT IS NOT MY RESPONSIBILITY:
generously and unconditionally love and respect myself and others.	if others don't love and respect me the way that I do myself.
take care of myself.	to take care of others without their permission.*

---

* *Children or other minor dependents are the obvious exception to this and some other boundaries presented here. The special case of parenting is a universe of its own to be taken up another time. Many of these same principles of softening attachment and honoring freedom apply, but the underlying responsibilities are distinct to that relationship.*

IT IS MY RESPONSIBILITY TO:	IT IS NOT MY RESPONSIBILITY:
listen, if I choose to enter into conversation.	whether or not others listen to me.
think, speak, and act in a way that is true to my heart.	what others think, say, or do, including how they respond to what I say or do.
acknowledge and honor my authentic feelings and experiences.	how others feel or to judge or condemn the authentic experience of others.
give counsel from my wisdom when invited (and I agree) to do so.	to give unsolicited advice.
cultivate my own understanding of the world and use my voice when I trust that my intentions and methods are wise.	how others understand the world or the opinions they express about it.
be honest.	whether or not others are honest.
remain in integrity with myself and my truest intentions.	how others define integrity or to decide whether or not they are being true to themselves.
live my values.	when others act on different principles than I do.

IT IS MY RESPONSIBILITY TO:	IT IS NOT MY RESPONSIBILITY:
refrain from violence in thought, word, and action, which includes blame, gossip, and insults.	when others cultivate harmful thoughts or choose to engage in blame, gossip, or insults.
remain in love, not fear, freeing myself of my own limiting thoughts.	if others are fearful or unloving. However others may be engaging in relationship, it is the best they are capable of at that time, perhaps constrained by their own limiting thoughts.
acknowledge the unique differences in each person.	if others choose not to acknowledge differences.
choose the people with whom I have relationships.	if others choose not to have a relationship with me.
continue learning, growing, and evolving as my life unfolds.	if others don't believe they have more to learn or resist change and evolution in their life.

These are the boundaries of boundless love, the scaffolding of relationships in which we honor one another as we are in all our wondrous possibilities.

REFLECTION: Witnessing Your Relationships

Now that we have explored some of the contours of attached, codependent love and the parameters we might redefine as a pathway to a freer (and perhaps more sustainable) approach, you are invited to return to the rich and distinct details of your own life and relationships. Taking a look at the juxtaposed recommendations above, perhaps consider the ways in which you may have denied some of the responsibilities I have suggested you might adopt on the left-hand side. You might also consider ways that you have intruded on the responsibilities of others listed on the right-hand side. With minimal judgment, just look for some clear examples in your life where these lines have been crossed.

I'll get you started with some examples from my life. In just the past few weeks, I have:

- considered myself inadequate to truly love my wife and children.

- allowed basic health-promoting practices that I know serve me to lapse, like going for a few long walks a week.

- not truly heard my son as he expressed his very authentic and valid fears stemming from the fact that a tree fell on the roof above his bedroom during a snowstorm(!) (luckily neither he nor the roof was harmed).

- agreed to conversations with those I prefer not to associate with, believing my attention would be beneficial to them (how could it be, when coming from such a place of resistance?).

- harmfully gossiped about and insulted others.

- judged myself when others missed a class in a recent course I taught.

- believed myself responsible to clarify another's understanding of philosophical principles.

- given advice to someone when, long ago, I decided it was not in their or my best interest to continue doing so.

I could keep going. Here you can see how, despite my familiarity with what I believe to be appropriate, love-affirming boundaries in my relationships, this is an ongoing, moment-to-moment, lifelong practice. As a fellow human being, then, I invite you to be as freely honest with yourself as you can with this exercise. This is not about judging or scorekeeping. It's about beginning to bear witness to our habit patterns and behaviors and to cultivate the courage to mindfully choose where we place our next step.

Right Speech

To apply this spirit of softening attachments and establishing loving boundaries to our lives, I would like to invoke the Buddhist principle of right speech, one of the elements of the Eightfold Path. So much of how we relate to one another is transmitted in our words, however they are spoken, written, or otherwise communicated. This feels like an appropriate place to focus our attention and develop fresh tools. A variety of other teachings stem from, and are intermingled with, the basic principle of right speech, such as nonharming, nonviolent communication, and the Zen Peacemakers' Way of Council practice.

In the Buddhist tradition, there are four aspects of right speech: (1) honesty; (2) consistency (not "adjusting" the truth based on who our audience is); (3) refraining from cruelty; and (4) vocalizing equanimity by not unnecessarily dramatizing. Interwoven with this guidance is the underlying principle of mindfulness — we must be aware of the thoughts and judgments we are formulating so that we can understand the wisdom of the speech that might ensue. As a general rule of thumb, it's not a bad idea to speak a bit more slowly, pausing as necessary to ascertain our most heartfelt intentions.

As important as the words we say are the words we hear. Deep listening is the cornerstone of right speech. The archetype for this is the figure Kwan Yin, which means the one who hears the cries of the world. Often presented in androgynous form, statues of Kwan Yin typically have a face with a neutral affect. This represents the virtue of listening before we apply our judgments. So many of us simply want to be heard, making openhearted listening a deeply compassionate act, nourishing, as Thich Nhat Hanh wrote, "both speaker and listener." Sometimes the contribution we might aspire to make to the world is simply our attentive presence.

Mindfulness can also help us discern when the right time is to listen and when to speak. We are free to choose when we will lend our ear or tongue. Refraining from speech or from listening can often be the most compassionate next step, perhaps if we are feeling distracted or otherwise tending to our own needs. We can feel confident that we are serving the cause of loving-kindness when we say, "Can we pause this conversation for a while? I'm not able to give it the wise listening or speaking that it and you deserve."

In convening with fellow practitioners in the Zen Peacemaker tradition, often before we commence a volunteer activity, I have become familiar with the Way of Council practice. In this method, we stand or sit in a circle, typically using a bead or other small token to indicate whose turn it is to speak. When it's our turn, we are invited to say anything we believe warrants sharing. It can relate to our mood, what we were doing earlier that day, or anything else so long as it comes from our own experience. Passing the token without speaking is an equally honored choice.

The key to the Way of Council is that the other members of the circle practice listening without responding at all. There is no cross talk (responding directly to what another person has said), and we even intend to refrain from changing our facial expression, such as by grinning or frowning. This may feel a bit extreme, but I deeply appreciate this method of rebalancing our instinct to jump in with our judgment-laden responses, whatever they may be. We take up the posture of Kwan Yin and expand our capacity to listen with genuine compassion.

Another tributary stream to the teaching of right speech is validation, followed by curiosity. As one of the pediatric therapists we met with over the years told us about our children, "always validate," and that has become a mantra for me. A foundational step in fostering loving relationships is recognizing and honoring the experience of others. Then, before leaping to what we conclude is the best way to help, we can ask that person what they need.

For example, if my son is expressing disappointment about a below-average grade on a recent test, I might think it's my responsibility to help him feel better by saying, "It's not a big deal, son. Don't worry about it. I'll quiz you before your test next time." But that response is a subtle denial of how he's feeling in the moment and inserts my assumptions about what he needs. A more loving response might be, "I hear that you are disappointed by the grade on your test. I understand that can be disappointing. Is there anything that you want from me?" Very often we may find that, when people express their feelings to us, they are not looking for us to fix them. Our kind attention is all they need. We honor and empower them when we acknowledge their ability to decide what happens next.

The Traditional Loving-Kindness Meditation

Among mindfulness meditation and Buddhist practices, the metta, or loving-kindness, meditation is one of the most popular. Used as a means for cultivating love for ourselves and others, it typically expresses aspirations for happiness, avoidance of harm or difficulty, peace, and awakening. These phrases are repeated in a cycle that begins with us and extends to our friends and family, then to people we have conflicts with, and then to all beings.

There are numerous versions of this meditation, each with its unique translation and adaptation of these underlying themes. I offer you some examples to deepen your familiarity with the practice. When I first started meditating, I used phrases offered by Bhante Gunaratana in *Mindfulness in Plain English*:

- "May I be well, happy, and peaceful."

- "May no harm come to me."

- "May no difficulty or pain arise for me."

- "May I always meet with success."

In our practices at the Zen Center of Denver, we use these phrases, here extending them to those closest to us:

- "May my friends and family be happy."

- "May my friends and family be free from strife and disease."

- "May my friends and family be free from suffering."

- "May my friends and family be at peace."

As I engaged with this practice, I discovered that the meaning these words contain and my intentions in expressing them shifted over time. Often, I found that certain words did not resonate with me anymore or felt contrary to my deeper values and truth. During a virtual retreat I participated in as part of the Mindfulness Meditation Teacher Certification Program, I raised these concerns with my mentor, the accomplished mindfulness teacher Dalila Bothwell. She responded, "Oh, I don't like the metta phrases." What a relief! What a compassionate reminder that we are always free to adapt or put down these practices when our knowing recognizes that they are not serving us.

I want to extend to you this same freedom, which of course you already possess. The metta phrases provided above, and my latest iteration of them offered in the guided meditation below, are just my temporary expressions of an intention of loving-kindness. I invite you to explore them and trust you will use them, adapt them, and discard them as you define your own practice.

At times, for me, the metta practice can feel mechanical, and that's okay. We may still find that, after a few cycles of repeating them, our mind has cleared and our heart has softened. I sometimes repeat one of the verses quickly to myself while in the car if I'm stuck in a downward thought cycle or as I'm leaving a disappointing or frustrating encounter. Whatever the circumstance may be, I trust that my deeper intention is loving-kindness. Having these phrases close at hand helps me return to my heart center.

At other times, you might question the authenticity of what you are expressing in the meditation toward others, particularly those you conflict with. Practicing this meditation might prompt the opposite effect of what you intend: It reminds you of your animosity toward a person or the unrepaired harm you experienced with them. If such feelings arise for you, then it is always acceptable to pause rather than plow through. Those unintended feelings can become your practice at that moment. You can explore them just as they are and see what you find.

In the guided meditation to follow, I am offering my own twist on this loving-kindness practice, stemming from how my understanding and appreciation of it has evolved over time. Drawing from the inspiration underlying most of this book, I have substituted the aspirational phrases (e.g., "May I be…") with affirming ones (e.g., "I am…"). This has a twofold purpose for me. The first is practical: There is considerable evidence that when we state aspirations as already accomplished, our mind will begin to believe them and our behaviors will begin to reflect them. The second is more personal: I genuinely trust these phrases are always true for me and for you. Let's take a pause from all our searching for the truth of loving-kindness. Let's consider the possibility that it is already and always present, right here, free for us to give and receive anytime we open our hearts to it.

MEDITATION: Free Metta

Take a moment to settle into your seat. Settle and soften. Breathe. Welcome home.

Spend some time with your breath and its gentle ebb and flow. Let your mind drop down into your body's sensation of it.

Now we begin with offering loving-kindness to ourselves. We might recognize that an abiding love arises when we honor the deepest truth of who we are. Sitting here, we are utterly sufficient. Every piece of us, the brilliance and the wounds, the strength and the tenderness, is complete just as it is. While we may have needs, nothing is lacking. Nothing is separate.

If you are ready, please join me by repeating:

I am present.

I am whole.

I am worthy of love, joy, and ease.

I am free to greet the next moment with an open heart.

Now we turn to those closest to us:

My friends and family are present.

My friends and family are whole.

My friends and family are worthy of love, joy, and ease.

My friends and family are free to greet the next moment with an open heart.

And now to those we don't yet know:

Those I don't yet know are present.

Those I don't yet know are whole.

Those I don't yet know are worthy of love, joy, and ease.

Those I don't yet know are free to greet the next moment with an open heart.

And now to those we conflict with:

Those I conflict with are present.

Those I conflict with are whole.

Those I conflict with are worthy of love, joy, and ease.

Those I conflict with are free to greet the next moment with an open heart.

And now to all beings:

All beings are present.

All beings are whole.

All beings are worthy of love, joy, and ease.

All beings are free to greet the next moment with an open heart.

Rest for a moment. Breathing.

Now let us begin again:

I am present.

I am whole.

I am worthy of love, joy, and ease.

I am free to greet the next moment with an open heart.

Now we turn to those closest to us:

My friends and family are present.

My friends and family are whole.

My friends and family are worthy of love, joy, and ease.

My friends and family are free to greet the next moment with an open heart.

And now to those we don't yet know:

Those I don't yet know are present.

Those I don't yet know are whole.

Those I don't yet know are worthy of love, joy, and ease.

Those I don't yet know are free to greet the next moment with an open heart.

And now to those we conflict with:

Those I conflict with are present.

Those I conflict with are whole.

Those I conflict with are worthy of love, joy, and ease.

Those I conflict with are free to greet the next moment with an open heart.

And now to all beings:

All beings are present.

All beings are whole.

All beings are worthy of love, joy, and ease.

All beings are free to greet the next moment with an open heart.

And for the third time:

I am present.

I am whole.

I am worthy of love, joy, and ease.

I am free to greet the next moment with an open heart.

Now we turn to those closest to us:

My friends and family are present.

My friends and family are whole.

My friends and family are worthy of love, joy, and ease.

My friends and family are free to greet the next moment with an open heart.

And now to those we don't yet know:

Those I don't yet know are present.

Those I don't yet know are whole.

Those I don't yet know are worthy of love, joy, and ease.

Those I don't yet know are free to greet the next moment with an open heart.

And now to those we conflict with:

Those I conflict with are present.

Those I conflict with are whole.

Those I conflict with are worthy of love, joy, and ease.

Those I conflict with are free to greet the next moment with an open heart.

And now to all beings:

All beings are present.

All beings are whole.

All beings are worthy of love, joy, and ease.

All beings are free to greet the next moment with an open heart.

✦

There is no need to ask for presence, wholeness, worthiness, or freedom, for ourselves or others. They already belong to you and to everyone you know. With this meditation, we set aside the practice of requesting and engage the practice of remembering.

Chapter 8

Forgiving and Being Forgiven

*When everything falls apart and we feel uncertainty,
disappointment, shock, embarrassment, what's left is
a mind that is clear, unbiased, and fresh.*
— PEMA CHÖDRÖN, *When Things Fall Apart*

*Oh lord, to fail in heart, and each day grow more hollow,
Sometimes I just don't wanna know....
It's a seven-story mountain. It's a long, long life we live.
Got to find a light and fill my heart again.*
— RAILROAD EARTH, "Seven-Story Mountain"

Her pudgy, crisscrossed legs spilled out of the soft plastic chair on the floor, the type of chair that is designed to gently fit a baby's body. Wearing a pink onesie with yellow and blue flowers on it, she was clapping her hands and babbling to a tune that only she knew. My daughter loved these times sitting on the floor of the kitchen while her parents put groceries away or prepared the next meal.

I was standing at the stove, having just returned from my job at a law firm and hustling to boil some pasta. I needed to head back upstairs to my laptop "ASAP" to complete a memo that was due by "end of day." As I poured the coiled noodles into the pan, I heard her sing, "Bah. Bah. Bah." My mind was elsewhere, though, bouncing furiously among the arguments I was going to weave into the document, my fear of missing the deadline, and that volatile haze of thoughts that was a perpetual torrent in my twentysomething life.

"Bah. Bah. Bah," she bleated tenderly.

I strained the noodles into the colander and emptied the red sauce into a porcelain bowl, punched the time on the microwave, and hit Start.

"Bah. Bah. Bah."

As I pulled the sauce out of the microwave and mixed it with the pasta, a bit of its bright red spilled on the counter and onto the floor. Instantly, my haste and anxiety yielded to frustration and anger.

"Bah. Bah. Bah."

"Eleanor, be quiet!!" I shouted into the air — at no one at all, really. The sharp, piercing sound was a surprise to us both.

I remember the next moments as if they were in slow motion. I turned to look at my precious six-month-old and watched as her bright, lucid blue eyes began to squint, and then as her brow began to fold. Her nose wrinkled and then the corners of her lips curled downward. Gradually, her body recoiled as if it had suffered a blow and her eyes, pink and then red, began to shed tears. She opened her mouth and cried out into the still air of the room. Her cheerful melody had turned to shame; her safety had been jeopardized; her seamless attachment to her dad had been disrupted.

This was the first time I recall harming my daughter. Tragically for both of us, there was more times to come.

Later, I was sitting with my family at a casual restaurant. We had brought our precious son home from China a few years earlier, and he was pursuing his meal in his typical buoyant fashion: our ten-foot radius was blanketed with rice and crumbs; his lips and cheeks were shellacked with sauce; the drumbeat of his babbling, shrieks, and hearty guffaws filled the restaurant.

Rather than enjoying his circus-like display of joy and ease, the kind perhaps only a child can create, I was monitoring my internal thermometer of how much I could bear of this mess, noise, and perceived intrusion on the meals of those around us. Never mind that the other diners did not exhibit the slightest concern over his behavior; my management of this situation was about my standards as a father and my identity as a parent.

My son then lofted the jagged remaining half of his blueberry muffin across the table and onto the floor. Having bought in wholeheartedly to my strategy of decisive action to correct bad behavior, I pounced. Leaping up from my seat, I gruffly and swiftly extracted him from his chair and sprinted with him in my arms into the nearby bathroom. Carrying him into a stall, I closed the door and began to dictate, for the hundredth time, my expectations of how he should act in a restaurant. While my definitions may have been defensible, my delivery was not. My lips were snarled and my tone was vicious. I was "sick and tired" of having this discussion, I said, as I pointed my dictatorial finger in front of his face, the energy of its condemnation cutting through him.

My son, confused by this performance, one he has seen many times before, and unconvinced that my rigid container of rules and restrictions suited him, began to shout back. He wasn't articulating counterpoints, of course, he was just mirroring my tone in volume and derision. Once on this path of escalation, I was ill-equipped to find an off-ramp. My voice rose further into the realm of hysterics and then that accusing, reprimanding finger thrust forth and struck him on his chest, right about where his heart must have been. He was not quite three years old.

In the silence that followed, he stared blankly at me, one of the two people he had grown to utterly depend on — had no choice, really, but to — and I began to recognize what I had done. The fact that I had touched my son in anger began to sink in. For all the books I had read and classes I had attended, dreams I held and fantasies I visualized of being a good father, I had now crossed a line that I knew, for me, without any shade of doubt or ambiguity, was wrong. Very, very wrong. And now it was too late to take it back.

I began to grovel. "I am so sorry, son. I should not have hit you like that. That was wrong. I am so, so sorry." He was still just as confused. My wild, rapid change in tone and emotion was beyond his young mind's capacity to digest. What I suspect he did know, though, was that he had been harmed. His chest hurt. After a few more moments of me attempting to repair and reconcile with him, I sheepishly led him back to our seat outside the bathroom door and sat down with my family.

"We could hear you," my wife said. "I think everyone in the restaurant could."

And there it was. The universe had seen me. And I was a monster.

The Well of Grace

What do we do with our mistakes? In an important way, they are indelibly imprinted on those we have harmed. There is no way to completely erase them. The same is true for the harm we have suffered through the actions of others. It is futile to pretend that we can shed them entirely or ignore them as we proceed through life.

The challenge arises, however, when we let these regrets prevent us from realizing our freedom to live with a loving heart. Clinging to mistakes as we do, we perpetually punish ourselves or others in the belief that this pattern somehow resolves these errors. We persuade ourselves that transcendence can only be achieved when our suffering matches the damage that has been inflicted. Eventually, we accrue these faults as emblems of our identities, which only condemns us to repeat them. The guiltier we feel, the more prone we may be to play out this cycle, trapping us in the past and banning us from grace. This is how we *more* our regrets.

Forgiveness — the mindful practice of lessening our attachment to unhealthy cycles of shame or blame — is the heart of the empty path. Guilt over our mistakes and resentment toward others may be our greatest barriers to living free. As we struggle to stay on the thin surface of our perfectionism, powered by the centrifugal force of avoiding our innermost shame, we find it difficult to forgive. At the heart of the difficulty is our faith that those of us who have perpetrated harm do not deserve forgiveness. And that means all of us.

Forgiveness, then, is perhaps the ultimate emotional turnaround. It's an about-face on our static, lifelong belief that the appropriate response to harm is perpetual suffering.

It's the final release of our most deeply held attachments — to our regrets, our shame, and our innermost identity. "To obtain that which we have not, we must go by the way that we know not," said Saint John of the Cross. To realize true forgiveness, to finally free ourselves from the otherwise endless cycle of shame and regret and regression, we must be willing to walk a different path.

In this way, forgiveness is an act of tremendous courage. It is brave to forgive. In our traditional mindset, we might think of forgiveness as weakness, as a denial or a bypassing of the underlying harm involved (or, worse, an endorsement of it), and as a careless escape from our most important responsibilities. It is, in fact, the very opposite of these things. In order to forgive authentically, we must acknowledge the full expanse of what we or others have done, the sometimes immeasurable harm it has created, and identify the most honest and compassionate steps to take to repair and remedy these to the best of our ability.

In our heart of hearts and truth of truths, we are all inherently forgiven. We are all innately worthy of love and belonging. The well of grace is never empty; it awaits, ready to nourish our capacity to create peace in our hearts and in our world. To realize this, though, and to enter the peace and liberation of the empty path, we must be willing to witness, embody, and act on this inspiration. And often that is not easy.

What Forgiveness Looks Like

Returning to my experience parenting my precious children, what might forgiveness look like? The harm of those mistakes is real; it is still present in the cells and sinews of my children's body-minds and certainly in mine. It can never be truly erased. These things I have done and cannot undo.

But what to do next? What path do I follow to cultivate my ability to enter the next moment with love and compassion, in this case to be a better parent? How do I relate to what I did back then so I can honor the truth of those I harmed and myself now?

As with so many features of our life and this path, forgiveness is not an instantaneous realization that "fixed" me and allowed me to reside permanently in a place of resolution and peace. It is truly a daily, lifelong practice, and it has included therapy, life coaching, deep grieving, meditation, testing new techniques, and so on, ad infinitum. It has ebbed and flowed and waxed and waned. It has included moments of satisfaction and moments of despair. Meanwhile, new mistakes and new harm continue to arise. And so do new opportunities for forgiveness.

When forgiveness is present, though, when I allow it to arise, I am free to see my children as they are and respond to them as they come forth. Having honored the past, I am no longer imprisoned by it. There is ease and joy in our interactions. There may be boundaries and enforcement of those boundaries — limits on screen time, redirection back to the homework, and exploration of a foul confrontation with a friend — but they are implemented with tenderness and love. My voice is soft and my stomach and shoulders are relaxed. My children have their space to grow, and I am here to witness, support, and enjoy it.

Today the sun comes up, and I start again.

REFLECTION: Where Are You Withholding Grace?

You are invited now to pause and consider areas in your life where grace may be calling but you have not yet answered. Starting with another person, consider someone who has harmed you in ways you are not yet able or willing to forgive. Name the person. What did they do that caused this harm you feel, which is authentic and valid? Take a moment to describe some of these incidents in detail.

As always, please practice discernment, recognizing events that may be too traumatic to investigate right now. Before you have had the chance to practice these techniques and, even then, perhaps in the absence of qualified professional support, revisiting some of our most grievous wounds can unintentionally deepen them. Cultivate your wisdom and compassion to choose areas of your life that you feel comfortable working with today.

Turning the lens inward now, perhaps explore an action that you have taken, words you have spoken, and thoughts you have harbored that you believe harmed others. Name those people and describe the incidents, taking up just one in detail for now. Our own offenses can be as painful to revisit as the ones others have perpetrated against us, so here too please be patient and alert in your exploration. Walk gently as you take these first steps of forgiveness.

Empty Mistakes

"All beings are by nature Buddha," wrote Zen master Hakuin. Nothing is excluded. When the Buddha realized the emptiness of all modes of experience, which precipitated his supreme enlightenment, mistakes and their accompanying regrets were not left out. Nothing is separate from this underlying truth. Yet our relationship to mistakes, in which we abide in regret or blame and deny forgiveness, will continue in its endless cycle as long as we believe they are separate from us, possessing a permanence and inherent identity that is distinct from our own.

We can look at any incident in our past to understand it this way, just as we have done with the chair, the kalamata olive, and other people. Perhaps reference your description of a regrettable event that you explored in the last section. Looking at all the details, the factors and circumstances, the material elements and all the accompanying thoughts and considerations, and extending the possible penumbrae of impact outward into the future, including how it lives in your and others' hearts today, ask yourself: "Which of these aspects makes that mistake what I believe it to be?"

We absolutely must be careful here. The harm enacted on us and that we have created in the world is real. It may well have been wrong in every conceivable way. It may have generated tragic, even horrific consequences and warrant dedicated and deliberate action to remedy it. That is all completely valid, as is the way these events resonate in your body and mind today. And, at the same time, with all this completely and equally true, it is also true that our mistakes are empty.

Does this mean we can ignore them? No. Please, no. Regret, shame, blame, and bitterness are the manifestations of separation, which is denial of the full breadth of the truth of these experiences. The response to our mistakes, as we awaken to their emptiness, is reconciliation. It is practicing the art, as difficult and distant as it may sometimes be, of reunifying the fact of these experiences with the always true fact of our and others' inherent wholeness. We have done many things that we ought not have done, and so has everyone else. To embrace our freedom and responsibility in the next moment, to break the cycle of these habit energies, we must learn to see that, all the while, we abide in the peace of emptiness, which the world cannot give or take away. We are unblemished, always completely forgiven. Our next step may include remedy and repair, but what is there, in fact, to regret?

Cause and Effect Are One

Buddhist teachings about karma can offer us a helpful means of exploring the contours of forgiveness and how it applies to our usual cycles of harm and regret, violation and contempt. On the surface, and as often described in popular culture, karma can seem like some universal moral justice system that maintains a balance between errors and their consequences. "Karma is gonna get you," we might say, as the driver cuts us off or our friend betrays us.

More precisely, though, karma is simply an acknowledgment of the mechanisms of cause and effect. If I slam my hand down on my desk right now, it will make a loud smacking sound, my hand will sting, and I will probably feel like a fool. If I refrain from watering the plant on my windowsill, it will eventually die. That's the law of cause and effect, and nothing escapes its functioning.

At the same time, as we have explored, every person, place, thing, incident, and idea arises from innumerable and, ultimately, unknowable causes and conditions. The path that each element followed to arrive at its infinitesimal moment of being is galactic in scope, and each of them is dependent on every other to create the new thing or event that is arising now. Nothing can exist without everything. Every single thing is contingent on all things. Like the endgame of Jenga, if you pull one block out, the whole structure falls.

In this way, we might see that causes and effects, like all other aspects of life, despite their apparent multiplicity, are inherently unified. We have been trained to view and treat things as possessing a permanency and an identity that separate them. There is a seed over here and dirt over there and rain up above and now comes this new tree. Each appears to be isolated and distinct. But when we explore the emptiness of each of these things, including their innumerable and ultimately untraceable causes and conditions, what separates them then? In fact, they are co-arising in a breathtaking miracle of interdependence that we can only pretend to understand. The all contains the one, and the one contains the all. William Blake was right. We can see all things as they are: infinite.

If we can glimpse beneath the veneer of separateness, karma and its attachments dissolve, cause and effect are re-unified, and each moment is born anew. Where does that leave us? Free. Free to greet the next moment and respond to it with our truest, most heartfelt intentions. Forgiveness arises of its own accord.

REFLECTION: Revisit Your Regrets

You are invited to return now to your description of grievances and regrets. Selecting one, perhaps consider what aspects of them feel unresolved and what action you might take to address that. Maybe you need to explore it in more detail or share your feelings with a trusted friend. Eventually, you might decide that you need to revisit the issue with the person who harmed you or the one to whom you have caused harm (a possibility we will explore more later). There may be need for professional support like therapy. In these cases, perhaps prioritize what will serve you and your integration of this event or concern with the rest of your whole and loving life.

Relatedly, you might consider the ways in which harboring your regrets or anger about these events serves your purpose of awakening to peace and freedom. I encourage you to write these down as fluidly as you can. These are all valid expressions of the benefit you see in your feelings about these important events in your life. Take some time to explore them. You are not pretending to "let them go"; these events will always be with you in some way.

Now just imagine: How might your thinking about these events evolve in your ever-renewing life? What would it be like if you put them down for a while? What do you need to be at peace? How can the abundantly resourced person that is you shape your relationship with these offenses in a way that serves you and all beings? Just imagine.

The Art of Lessening Mistakes

How do we find peace in our lives while acknowledging harm? This is a difficult journey, fraught with the pitfalls of repression or bypassing as well as blame or shame. Let us proceed carefully, with love, honoring all that is true for us in our experience of these events, while still opening ourselves to the possibility of the abiding peace and love that we deserve. For me, turning toward my most egregious mistakes, such as the parenting anecdotes I described at the outset, as well as my deepest grievances, such as the ones I might harbor from my childhood, has been the spark that lit my entry into this generous, illuminating path, from therapy and self-reflection, to conversations and journaling, and ultimately to meditation and Zen.

Let us turn first to the pain we carry and perhaps resentment we maintain toward those who have harmed us. As with many of our other practices, it can be most helpful to start with something that we can hold more lightly: an ill word from a colleague, a spurned effort at romantic attention many years ago, a sharp disagreement, an invite we didn't get, or another's error that cost us a setback in our career.

In these cases, revisiting the teachings in the previous chapters, we can begin to parse the facts of what that person did, validate our initial responses, and begin to think critically about how our ongoing emotional relationship to the event is serving us. As we sit here today, who is responsible for how we feel about the incident? What lingering power are we affording that person by carrying ill emotions about the event with us into the new moments of our life? We may bear no responsibility at all for what happened then, but what is our appropriate share of responsibility for how we experience it now? This is not a responsibility we owe to anyone other than ourselves.

Put another way, how have we added more to our grievances than they deserve? And how can we lessen their weight so that we might enter the next moment with the freedom of an open heart?

One of the many challenges that may arise with this effort can be that, when we soften our feelings of anger, resentment, or blame for just a moment, we may see that, underneath them lie more tender feelings and needs that have gone unsatisfied. Perhaps there is our need for acceptance and belonging, or for peace and security, or for love. We deserve all these things, and yet others may seek to deny our access to them. Holding yourself with compassion, allow space to explore these underlying feelings that may be intertwined with your memory of these harms. These are wounds that only you can mend. True forgiveness of others, which is ultimately a means of serving — even protecting — us, often requires a heightened degree of tenderness and vulnerability.

Next the invitation is to turn toward the person or group that harmed you. Resourcing yourself with the skills and understanding we explored in the chapters about love and compassion, as well as your mindful presence with things as they are, imagine facing those you blame and resent. You can begin by seeing their particularities, the material facets of them that you can observe, the way that they have come forth into your life. These experiences and observations are completely valid. They are yours, and they are real.

Honoring these observations, you can also intend to shift your perspective to the underlying truth of the other person. Perhaps recall our strategies of looking at them as a newborn infant or an empty canoe. You might imagine the story you have told yourself about the person and then reimagine it to remind yourself of how subjective and impermanent the story may be. You can imagine, as with all things, the innumerable and unknowable causes and conditions for this person's existence and for their behavior.

Please make no mistake: They are responsible and they are accountable. Their *actions* may not deserve forgiveness, ever. Is it also possible to witness, at the same time, a facet of them that is worthy of love? Is there a part of each of us that the tragedies of this world, including those we have caused, cannot tarnish? If you cannot affirm this yet, perhaps you can believe that someday you might.

A key next step might be to communicate your experience of this event to the other person. It could include a request that they take some action to repair the harm or prevent it in the future. In either case, it is vital to bear in mind that they may not recognize your experience of this situation or they may deny your request, either directly or passively. Whatever action you decide to take, an essential part of the practice is to soften your expectations of how the other person will respond. You only get to choose how you come forth in a way that honors your truest intentions. That's the boundary of your responsibility here.

As I hope you can see, this process is not about self-denial or sacrifice. It is not about wanting to "forgive and forget." This is about a genuine, deep exploration of your experience and ongoing feelings and emotions relating to it, then discerning your own best next step forward. As the embodiment of love and compassion, freedom and responsibility that you are, where does your path of forgiveness lead you now?

I want to acknowledge here that, even though I've recommended starting with a less complex event, there may well be far more serious and harmful wrongs that others have perpetrated against you. They could involve physical or emotional abuse or violence. They may entail injustice or other forms of oppression, either directed at you personally or at a group you are part of.

With these things in mind, try to prioritize the principle that forgiveness toward a person or group that perpetuates profound harm is not about repression and it is not about permission or endorsement. With forgiveness, we are not conceding that what was done is acceptable in any way or, worse yet, that we are somehow responsible for what transpired. We can practice forgiveness and keep in place our boundaries of safety and care. We can also consider whether additional action is necessary to prevent further harm to us or to others.

As we walk this path, we may find that forgiveness is ultimately not about a past event or another person. It is not about whether they have requested or deserve our forgiveness. It is not about whether our practice can undo the past or change how others behave in the future. It involves our recognition both that those people and circumstances are real, valid, and distinct and that nothing, including them, is separate from our truest self. In this way, forgiveness is about realizing our freedom to awaken to our life in all its illumination, no matter what external factors might impose themselves as obstacles on our path.

As with every aspect of the empty path, this is a life practice. Yes, the underlying truth of you and all beings is always present. At the same time, the realization of our inherent forgiveness and the application of it to our deepest difficulties usually unfolds gradually. Forgiveness may not be accessible to you at certain times or in certain situations. By attempting to stay open to the wide array of feelings involved with this practice, we can expand our capacity to forgive. We simply set out, again and again, to soften the weights we carry, and we trust that the peace of forgiveness can arise for us anew.

REFLECTION: Write a Letter

One of the most powerful practices I have done to lessen my attachment to the harm I have suffered due to another's actions is to write a letter to that person. I invite you now to take up one such situation in your life and write a letter to the person or group that has committed wrongs against you. You might begin by describing the facts of the events as best as you can recall them, in as much detail as possible. Then you might explore the impact on you of these actions, words, and events, whether they be physical, emotional, social, financial, or otherwise. You can go on to describe how these impacts have affected other, perhaps ongoing, aspects of your life. This is your opportunity to be as thorough as possible in processing the manifold ways these grievances have played out in your life, so please take some time and care with it.

In the last step, you can decide whether you will send the letter to its audience. I encourage you to pause the inclination to predict what their reaction will be or assume this process will yield any specific outcomes or changes in their behavior. Perhaps it will; perhaps it won't. The key question you might ask yourself is this: "Will sending this letter serve me and support my path to awakening and peace, regardless of what happens afterward?"

For me, in a particularly challenging instance, I realized I was not yet able to maintain full equanimity with what the outcome of sending such a letter would be. Instead, I read it aloud to my wife, who, fortunately for me in so many ways, has done her own work and training around nonjudgmental listening. Another very beneficial (and widely shared) practice is to direct your words at a spiritual figure you call forth in your mind. Pets can also be incredibly openhearted listeners.

You might also consider presiding over a ceremony. It can be just as powerful if you are the only participant. Read the letter aloud, let yourself experience the breadth of emotions and embodied feelings that it prompts, and then dispose of it. Maybe you'll burn it.

The Most Difficult Step: Forgiving Ourselves

Readiness to accept and forgive the fact we have created harm in the past is a vital step to generative transformation, perhaps *the* vital step. Our feelings of unworthiness and self-doubt can be the most daunting barriers to the peace and freedom we deserve. We may believe that we owe our mistakes and those we have wronged our unending remorse and suffering, thinking that may somehow atone for the damage we caused. Meanwhile, the shame we maintain can subconsciously lead us to repeat these cycles of harm and regret.

As with the other practices we have explored, applying emptiness to our mistakes can feel counterintuitive, contradictory, even callous or sociopathic. It may take a while before the seeds of doubt sprout into the growing suspicion that your beliefs and assumptions about you and your world are not serving you. Perhaps with forgiveness above all else, realizing our deepest nature and living in alignment with its truth requires us to put down our habit patterns and energies of the past. Saint John of the Cross whispers again: In order to change, we have to try something new.

Just as much with ourselves as with others, withholding forgiveness is a form of othering, of separating from the core unity of emptiness that we all share. It's also a means of denying aspects of ourselves — the parts we are unhappy with, embarrassed by, or afraid of. As we approach forgiving ourselves, then, we begin with a heartfelt acknowledgment of what happened, in all the specifics and details we can muster. As with our thoughts, other people, and every feature of our life, lessening our attachments is only possible after we fully recognize and reckon with all that the mistake is and means for us.

In the guided meditation to follow, I will escort you through each phase of this self-forgiveness journey. Here are some of the core elements to keep in mind for your practice:

- Identifying the specific event to work with, with grace and discernment for what feels healthy and fulfilling to address at that moment.

- Acknowledging and naming the aspects of the situation, including your thoughts, judgments, and bodily sensations of it.

- Recognizing the underlying emotions that are intertwined with this experience, including those you may be inclined to reject or ignore.

- Investigating the causes and preconditions, circumstances, and factors that led to that event, both the external physical components and the internal, mental, and emotional ones.

- Seeing the vast expanse of elements that comprise this situation, considering again the manifold pieces of you, then asking yourself: "Might there be space for this to pass through?"

- Affording yourself compassion and grace: This can be a painful and difficult process, and it is best to traverse it carefully, discerning your best next step forward.

- Affirming your inherent worthiness of love, peace, and freedom, that is, your worthiness of forgiveness.

- Stating your regret aloud and then, patiently, that you forgive yourself.

- Acknowledging that you are forgiven, peering into the next moment to discover any additional action that may be calling you to address the situation in a way that serves you and your intention to offer loving peace to the world.

This last step is an important one. With true forgiveness, the clarity of our best next step can shine brighter. Where there is harm, there may need to be repair. In pursuing that, it may help to set aside expectations of atonement, the idea that there is a certain weight to your offense that can be counterbalanced with a precise measure of grief, compensation, or effort. How could we ever know where the right balance rests for us, for the others involved, and for all beings? That is not an excuse for inaction, but it is license to proceed authentically without attachment to expectations for a certain outcome. Reckoning calls to us and, if we don't respond with our truest intention, we will not find peace.

Beyond the immediate next steps, there can also be an abiding commitment to prevent future harm from playing out in a similar way. Here is a brief statement you might reference to vocalize your commitment to such a path: "I see that I have caused harm. I see the pain it has created. With love for myself and all beings, I commit to repairing this harm and the wounds in my own heart. To abandon this cycle of injury and regret, I vow to take conscious steps to prevent similar harm from arising again, to the very best of my ability."

For all these forgiveness practices, including the guided meditation to follow, you will probably find that you need to return to specific incidents, memories, and beliefs again and again. This is usually not a "one and done" exercise, and that is okay. This is the lifelong practice of forgiveness, and we may find that it's possible to gradually lighten our attachment to these regrets, the shame they have inspired, and the habit patterns they enable. This faith is the practice of the Third Noble Truth: There is the resolution of suffering. You are invited to believe that it can be so.

MEDITATION: Forgiveness Ceremony

Take a moment to settle into your seat. Arouse your intention to create a space of safety and peace. Perhaps allow yourself several deep breaths to cleanse your heart and mind.

Attuning to your body, consider letting the small hook on the crown of your head gently lift you into a posture of nobility. You are doing something important. This is sacred time.

Awakening to the natural rhythm of your breath, feel how it is rising and falling in your body. Just notice its gentle ebb and flow. Let the breath find parts of you that are not yet settled into this loving place. Give those areas a moment of kind attention.

Now you are invited to consider an action you have taken in the past that is a source of regret for you — perhaps some harsh words, reckless behavior, or even a violent act. It may have caused harm to you or to others. Maybe it involved dishonesty, anger, or carelessness. You may have done it knowingly or unknowingly, intentionally or unintentionally. Please identify the action that is calling you to work with it right now.

Perhaps begin by acknowledging that this event did occur. It is a real part of your life. You might confirm its presence with a soft "This I have done." This I have done.

Next, breathing in your inherent strength, do your best to examine all aspects of this incident. Where did it happen? Who was present? What did it sound, look, and feel like? What do you know or remember about this through your direct experience of it? As difficult as it may be, with as much courage as you can, revisit it as completely as possible.

Please also be compassionate with yourself. If the pain of remembering this event becomes too hard to bear, give yourself space to pause, breathe, and hold yourself. It may sometimes be necessary to stop this inquiry for now; discernment is an important part of the practice. Perhaps return another time to a less severe memory, which will help you build capacity to work with more challenging ones later.

As you inquire into the nature of this episode, consider how it feels in your body, right now, as you remember it. What thoughts arise for you as you explore this memory? What judgments, heaviness, or confusion arises? You might name the feelings and emotions that are present for you right now. Perhaps "sad, sad," "aching, aching," "ashamed, ashamed."

Voyaging further still, it may be helpful to consider: What aspects of your personality — your story of you — do you associate with this event? How is your sense of identity intertwined with the action you took? Again, you are invited to name this gently to yourself. Perhaps "I am an angry person." "I am reckless." "I can be cruel to the people closest to me." Be sure to breathe, maintaining both your steadiness and your tenderness. Be patient with this moment. Give these feelings their due.

Now look below the surface. What fears or sorrows might you notice if you look beneath all the ideas you have about yourself and this incident? What do you feel is lacking? What unattended needs or longings are present? What wounds do you carry that are also a part of this experience?

Maybe ask yourself, "What parts of my life have I tried to separate from? What aspects of myself have I denied?" Breathe, my dear friend. Breathe. You are safe. You might tend to yourself by putting a kind hand on your heart. For example, I might whisper to myself, "It's okay, Billy. It's okay, dear."

Now we might restate what we have done in a new way, keeping ourselves held: "I see what I have done. I see its many details and the numerous feelings I have about it. I see the harm it has caused others and myself, some of which I may never fully know or understand. I see there are numerous conditions from which this event arose, from within me and around me. There it all is. I see it now."

Sitting here, in your place, with your breath, seeing the entirety of this experience as best you can, perhaps be open to the possibility that there is space for it all here. As much as it may swirl and stab, smolder and spark, you need not and cannot contain it. Let it swirl. Let it smolder. If this doesn't feel possible right now, perhaps consider believing that someday it can.

Now you might take the next step, saying, "Whatever I have done, however much harm I have caused, I am worthy of love. I am worthy of forgiveness." You may struggle to know this right now, and that's okay. You are still invited to say it to yourself. I know you can believe it. It is true. You are worthy of love. You are worthy of forgiveness.

Now we say this together, from across time and space: "I am sorry for what I have done. I am so very sorry." Say it in your heart to the person you have harmed. Say it to yourself. "I am sorry."

And now, patiently, with love: "I forgive myself now."

"I forgive myself."

All beings of the world and of all time, they hear you now. The tapestry of people, the birds, the streams, and the stars: They see you as you are right now. And they believe you.

Now we continue by affirming: "I am forgiven." "I am forgiven."

Forgiven.

Forgiven.

Hold yourself with love. Wrap your caring arms around yourself. Your flame shines brightly in this moment. Slowly, gently, let these thoughts and emotions begin to settle. Gradually, just let them rest. Come back to your refuge in the breath. Come back to this place you are in.

Soon you will get up and proceed with your precious life. This is your birthplace of peace. There may well be more action to take, repairs or remedies to seek, acknowledgment and nurturing to offer. Trust that you can abide in these. Perhaps trust that, whatever comes, you can proceed with love — love for yourself and for all the many beings of this tender world.

✦

You are invited to adapt this guided meditation for the practice of forgiving others, modifying it where you deem appropriate. As explored earlier in this chapter, you may find authentic inspiration to address the situation with the others involved, perhaps by relaying your experience of it or requesting action on their part. A key difference between posing these next steps to others versus committing to them ourselves is that, in the former case, we don't have any control over what happens next. Be that as it may, in whichever direction we are heading, we are free to take the action that we believe serves us best.

It may be beneficial to carry with you this brief mantra when you find yourself cycling into thought loops of shame about yourself or bitterness toward another. If it feels true, or you can believe that it might be, you can whisper: "I forgive you now" or "I am forgiven now." You are gently releasing the weight, heavier at first and now perhaps becoming much lighter, of an unchangeable past to create the beauty of an undiscovered future.

Chapter 9

Abandoning the Ego Self

*All suffering...arises from a mistaken understanding
that we are a separate and distinct self.*
— Tara Brach, *Radical Acceptance*

*I learned that to feel completely myself, 100%, is a different
feeling than usual, and that really being myself is
a state where "self" disintegrates.*
— Mike Gordon, *Doniac Schvice* newsletter

The first time I tasted alcohol was at Madeline Stark's
house. Her parents were out of town, and a large gathering of people from my high school was milling about her
backyard. Music was playing lightly, while the thick wall of
pines surrounding the yard dampened the bluster of all our
peacocking around the party. A childhood friend and fellow
ninth grader was holding a Corona bottle, and I asked for a
sip. Self-consciously lifting the bottle to my lips, I stifled a
grimace as the lukewarm bitter bubbles swirled in my mouth
and down my throat. So began my twenty-five-year love affair with booze.

In those adolescent days, as I encased myself in armor

as the turmoil in my life swirled around me, stirred with a healthy serving of good old-fashioned social awkwardness, alcohol became my most trusted companion. What began as a mild soothing of my anxious nerves quickly transformed into a prominent and beloved feature of my personality. My high school friends kidded (affectionately, I think…) that I gave off "Ted Kennedy vibes." Inspired by the story of Dr. Jekyll and Mr. Hyde, my college pals dubbed my drunken nighttime persona Mr. Wynne, the evil, uninhibited alter ego of my typically soft-spoken, reserved self: Dr. Billy. Looking for ways to fit in and to please, I embraced these shticks so much that I forgot they were social devices; they became my identity. With that self-image in place, I stepped into adulthood.

Over the next twenty years, I experienced most of the highs and lows that this toxic chemical has to offer, tangoing through life with alcohol as an eager partner. As with other codependent relationships, it consumed my mind. Every day, I would map my dissipation plan: when would I start, which features of my carefully curated wine and beverage collection would call to me, what was on the drink menu at the restaurant we might visit that night, and how I would measure my alcoholic portions and savor their flavors.

Of course, as it flowed into my brain, alcohol dominated our cohabitation there too. Elbowing aside my better intentions for presence, calm, and authentic connection with others, I welcomed in my inner drinking buddy, the one who returned alcohol's affection at the expense of the people around me, celebrated its vices as I exorcised my demons, and succumbed to its tempting anesthesia. As I descended into a stupor, or nursed my exasperated hangover, I missed classes and work meetings, opportunities for new, meaningful friendships, and the simple joys of being attuned to my children as we played together. My fraying marriage dangled by a thread. Meanwhile, eerily, I knew all along that my drinking was really just about one thing: erasing my authentic self and expediting my transition into oblivion. By more-ing my life with alcohol, I was actually annihilating it.

Then, as they do, things started to change. I embarked on the path of mindfulness and then Zen. As my mental gymnastics of trying to reconcile my drinking habits with this path grew more dubious, I began the practice of taking *jukai*, the lay ordination process in which one adopts the bodhisattva precepts and deepens their commitment to the Buddhist path. The student reflects on the sixteen precepts, cultivates their understanding of them, and authors a heartfelt vow to uphold each one in their own way. At the end, we receive a *rakusu*, a patched cloth that we sew and can hang around our neck while meditating, to symbolize a monk's robe.

The fifth precept states (in the translation used at the Zen Center of Denver): "I vow not to misuse alcohol or drugs, but to keep the mind clear at all times." This is not an edict for all Zen students to stop consuming alcohol or drugs. The principle is posed to the student, and the student generates their own understanding of how it applies to their life. For me, though, the fifth precept had my number. I could see it coming from a mile away. It was like that scene in *International Man of Mystery* when Austin Powers is escaping from Dr. Evil's underground lair. On the left side of the screen you see him driving a steamroller, on the right is a security guard, letting out a long scream as the steamroller very slowly inches toward him, as if he were incapable of avoiding it, "Ahhhhhhh." That was me and the fifth precept.

I knew that if I were going to give an authentic response to it, if I were going to be in integrity with it and myself, then the only possible thing for me to do was stop drinking alcohol. That was January 2019. Everything is always changing, and that was a big change for me.

My use of alcohol was intimately intertwined with the great lies of the self: that I am not worthy of joy, that I am not capable of peace, that I cannot stand face-to-face with truth. By finally dropping this aspect of my identity, I shed an important element of my idea of an ego self. With that weight lifted, the other layers of my identity onion got a little bit easier to peel back. This left the question, What's left at the center? Who or what am I, really?

The Beautiful Truth of Ourselves

For our whole lives, we have been trained to believe we are separate from others and the world around us. We embrace this way of thinking and set out to protect ourselves from harm and compete for the mental and material assets the world has to offer: information, wisdom, relationships, pleasure, money. All the while, we harden this perspective of ourselves as lacking, always in need of more to find satisfaction, perpetually fearing what we have acquired will be lost, or that disappointment, harm, or discomfort are lurking around the corner.

As we have explored, this is the essence of suffering: perpetual oscillation between craving and aversion and the futility of our efforts to satisfy these feelings. We have looked at this primarily from the perspective of the things we encounter: the places, people, thoughts, and emotions that arise through the course of our life. We have engaged with practices and ancient wisdom to glean some insight into their underlying emptiness and indivisibility from us and all beings. At the very heart of this problem, though, the root cause of all our suffering, is our very own self. It is our belief in this egoic self that isolates us and divides us from others and the world around us, spawning our attachments and fueling our perpetual dissatisfaction. It's time we turn our attention to it.

By investigating the self, we can discover its emptiness, what Buddhists refer to as no-self. As disorienting and perhaps unnerving as this may seem, walking these dimly lit steps ourselves is the only path to true liberation. When we realize our own emptiness and, in tandem, that of all other things, there is nothing left to attach to, fear, or crave. When there is no more gap between us and all that is, our persistent dissatisfaction is resolved, our efforts to feed our voracious ego with more are instantly obsolete. From this place we can greet our life with authentic peace and joy. It is not supernatural, but it is the holiest of things.

Living Unselfed

What does being "unselfed" look like in the real and practical milieu of our lives? Does it change the fact that we need to feed, educate, and support ourselves or choose to seek new friends and experiences? Does it mean we should abandon our families, responsibilities, and values?

I hope you can trust by now that it does not mean any

of these things. Softening and releasing our attachment to the ego self simply, albeit extraordinarily, changes our relationship to these many precious facets of our lives. We still go about our day with our feet on the ground, but the manifestations of our fear and craving — the anxiety about the upcoming meeting, the waxing anger about the traffic, our demands on and disappointment with those we love — mercifully diminish.

The Diamond Sutra text of the Buddhist tradition, as translated by A. F. Price, says, "Thus shall you think of all this fleeting world: a star at dawn, a bubble in a stream, a flash of lightning in a summer cloud, a flickering lamp, a phantom, and a dream." The material reality that surrounds us still presents itself, but the posture of our relationship to it changes from suspicious reservation to love, gratitude, and presence. Pain still arises — it always does — and so too sadness and loss, difficulty and tragedy, but we finally recognize that, even as we turn toward and honor these valid experiences, we need not be perpetually encumbered by them.

When we remember this truth during the day, our steps become a bit more buoyant and our grin curves a bit more easily. We are focused but unhurried, loving without controlling, and navigating each turn with our heart at the wheel. Quite the opposite from abandoning what we hold most dear, we are reimmersed in natural, authentic relationships with our friends and family, refreshed and joyful in our work and play, and resourced with courage and wisdom to confront the ills of our lives and this world. When we release the ideas of our identity as "must be this" and "have to be that," no one and no thing can harm us. Even the final mystery of death is powerless against us. The person it is coming for has already died.

REFLECTION: Define Yourself

Heady stuff, I know. Let's pause here and regroup. Perhaps get out your trusty pen and paper, those vital tools for decluttering the mind. You are invited now to describe yourself. You can start with your physical features as you see them now. You might list your values, your goals and aspirations, and some of your closest relationships. There is also your job, your hobbies, your location, and other aspects of your circumstance. Then there is your past, starting with your birth date and that whole luminous saga that unfolded since then with all its joy, sorrow, and change. You also might imagine your future, the array of horizons that might arise for you as you enter the next days and years. Take some care with this; do it with love.

Once you are satisfied that you have written enough, pause and look down at your words. You can embellish this exercise by taking out your ID or a photo of yourself nearby and putting it next to your pages. Maybe grab a slip of paper and write your full name down on it too.

Scan this collection and breathe. Feel into your body for a moment. Then come back up to your mind and ask yourself: "Is that me?"

The Buddha Way

A founder of Zen in Japan, Dogen, said, "To study the Buddha Way is to study the self. To study the self is to forget the self. To forget the self is to be actualized by myriad things." This is the succinct, timeless expression of our path of awakening, the empty path. It begins and ends with our self, the cause of all our suffering and the essential gateway to its ultimate resolution.

The legend of the Buddha's life is the archetypal story of this awakening. Born into the isolation and incredible comfort of life as a prince, he exited the palace walls and soon observed sickness, old age, and death — the emblems of pain in our world. Determined to free himself and others from suffering, he trained in the numerous practices taught at the time for attaining bodily ease and spiritual wisdom. His path took him to asceticism, the ultimate denial of worldly comfort and pleasure. Still not having found the lasting peace he sought, and on the brink of death from starvation, he realized the middle way of balancing the material and immaterial realms of life and took nourishment. Then he sat under a bodhi tree, determined not to get up until he had attained complete enlightenment.

Through the course of the night, the Buddha examined all aspects of himself, extending his search deep into his "past lives" and outward and ahead into his future ones. Meanwhile, numerous temptations of pleasure and the horrors of sorrow presented themselves to him. Exhausting all his seeking efforts, he was unable to find a semblance of the self to which he realized he had been so attached. On the cusp of this awakening, one last barrier stood in his way: self-doubt.

In the legend, this self-doubt is represented by Mara, the classical Buddhist deity, loosely akin to the devil. Mara comes to the Buddha and ridicules him, saying, "What makes you think you can experience supreme enlightenment? How can someone like you believe that you are worthy of that? Attain enlightenment right here and now, under this tree, as you sit? Really? You??" Does this sound familiar?

In response, the Buddha simply touched the ground, asking the earth and all beings of the world to bear witness to him. In response, all these myriad things — the people and plants, stones and stars — responded, thundering: *"You are worthy!"* With that, Mara, the spirit of the Buddha's last gasping self-doubt, was vanquished. No longer impeded, the Buddha looked up to see the morning star, and in it he saw the unimaginable peace of its emptiness and of his own. "Wonder of wonders," he proclaimed. "In this moment, I and all beings have attained awakening."

True Self Is No-Self

What did the Buddha realize in that moment? His story, after all, is your story. What might you realize in this moment, utterly worthy as you are? What insight did the morning star transmit to him? What truth does the dog on your lap, the pen on your table, or the soft pattern of your rug transmit to you?

We call it *emptiness*, for lack of a better word. I put it in the title of this book and have mustered my best efforts to explain what it might mean. All these teachings, bits of wisdom, and practices are really just different facets of this one all-encompassing jewel. At the heart of the jewel, the final step on the path, is the empty self.

The first step in understanding the concept of no-self is to consider our self-nature, the way we tend to think of ourselves as a unique persona in the world. The one who occupies space and traverses time, an unbroken chain that links what we were yesterday to what we are today and will be tomorrow. But if we pause to earnestly examine every syllable of this tale, we might struggle to identify which part of it truly constitutes the self to which we are so attached. Is it our physical body, our personality, or our biography? Isn't each one of these elements always changing, each one also composed of its own innumerable and unknowable sources, causes, preconditions, and components?

We will continue with this exploration in greater detail in the next sections of this chapter and in the guided meditation at the end. The punch line of this cosmic joke, though, is that after we have diligently peeled back every layer, painstakingly considered each and every element of our self, we aren't likely to find anything at the core. What are we, then? And what do we do next?

The beauty of recognizing no-self is that, in that instant, all the attachments we have clung to so desperately are dissolved. There is nothing to cling to and no one to do the clinging. The haze of regret, shame, anxiety, and fear dissipates, along with the debilitating burdens of insecurity and self-doubt. Arising anew in this moment, indivisible from all that is or ever could be, we enter into a kind of peace that the world cannot diminish. With a chuckle, we realize that it has been right here with us all along.

The Art of Lessening Yourself

Okay, you might be saying, if I am not me, then who was that person who drove to work yesterday? Who grew up in x town with y parents and graduated from z school? I don't know, is the honest answer, but it wasn't "you." Here's why.

The truth of impermanence — that everything is constantly changing — applies to us too. Heraclitus, the ancient Greek philosopher, expressed it well: "No person ever steps in the same river twice, for it's not the same river and it's not the same person." Isn't it the case that you too are always changing in both body and mind?

If you're of a certain age, you are growing. If you're of another, your bones and muscles are in decline. Your hair is growing or, if you're like me, it's falling out. You are radiating heat, even silently shedding skin. Perhaps more curiously, your mind has changed too. Your beliefs, your memories, your intentions, everything governing your outlook and experience of life is always evolving, responding to circumstances and in turn giving rise to new modes of thinking. Have you ever considered something you did, whether just yesterday or years ago, and thought to yourself, "The person I am now would never have said or done that. That's not me anymore?

Again adjusting our microscope of inquiry, we can see that, in every instant, our cells are undergoing rapid transformation. From our organs down to the tiniest fiber of our skin, they are doing the work of our body. At the same time, they are growing and shrinking, birthing and dying. The cells of our body completely replenish themselves every seven to ten years, at a pace of about 330 billion cells a day. So who was that person in your car yesterday, pressing the gas, turning the wheel, toggling the radio for a better song? We can't say. What was before and will be next is not what is now.

We can try to hang on, and try we do, but ultimately our thoughts and intentions can't change our truest nature, the same nature as that of the tree that's always changing outside our window.

In addition to impermanence, the other primary, deeply interwoven aspect of emptiness that we have investigated throughout this book is no-self: the lack of a core, abiding identity that makes something what we believe it to be. It's the nature of the chair, the kalamata olive, the Buddha, and you and me.

If I ask you who you are, you might wave your hands around your body and, probably growing a bit irritated, say, "Hey, I'm right here! This stuff right in front of you is me!" Taking a closer look, though, what part of you makes you you? Is it your hands and fingers, feet and toes? Your bones and sinews? Your internal organs? Surely those could come and go, be transplanted, and are always changing. They are not you.

What about your head, your brain, and its neurons? Is that really you in there? If you pardon the relatively absurd and perhaps gruesome thought, if someone else's brain was swapped in for yours, we might say, "There's Paul. He just had a brain transplant." You might be inclined to produce your driver's license or birth certificate or your name itself. Take a look at those, though. Are they you?

You might also point to your experiences, your memories, or your life story. You might say that your history is "you." As we know by now, though, that person in the past was not you, and moreover, the past is not real now. That's not exactly a safe haven for your selfhood. Here too, as with the chair, our concept of ourselves starts to reveal itself as just a convenient set of thoughts in our mind, which I think we can safely agree is not us.

As we approach the potential terminus of this monorail tour of our *self*, let me say a word about this thing we call consciousness, where some tend to arrive. Our current understanding of consciousness, the awareness that arises as the backdrop to our experiences, is relatively limited. Perhaps for this reason many teachers, including ones I greatly admire, have essentially deified it, correlating it to the concept of a soul or some other supernatural source. You might find support and inspiration in such beliefs as well, whether or not they're related to consciousness. It's not the purpose of this book to diminish or affirm faith-based or religious beliefs. My intention is to present you only with teachings and practices that we can all validate through our own inquiry, reason, and direct personal experience. Characterizations of consciousness that extend beyond its basis in the neurons and complex machinations of the brain, along with other supernatural beliefs, are immaterial to our investigation of the reality or unreality of the self.

So, then, what's left? If the self doesn't abide in our name and characteristics, our body, mind, experiences, or memories, then where is it? If you're able to discover where this self exists in space and time, a self that possesses a unique identity, separate from all other things, then please let me know! I've been looking for a long time and have yet to find it.

When it comes to defining who we are, perhaps the best we can honestly say is that we *are*. There's something here — a pure form of existence. Some have called it *thusness*;

German philosophers prefer the term *Dasein*, and I often use the dime store pamphleteer's *isness*. It's the reality of being beyond judgment or categorization. There is only one truth that is being, and being is the only true thing. One of my favorite songs invites us to "listen to the thunder shout: I am! I am! I am!" ("Let It Grow" by the Grateful Dead, for those who are curious.) Please join me in celebrating your I-am-ness. What more do we need than that?

Whatever words we might use to fill the empty space of "us," I encourage you to cultivate some comfort with the question. There's no need to rush to quench it with an answer just yet. I urge you to continue exploring your *self* on your own. It's one thing to understand these words on a page; it's quite another to realize them personally as your lived experience, your felt sense. Words are just like a finger pointing at the moon, as the Buddha said; they are not the moon itself. Don't read the menu; eat the food. As I have emphasized from the beginning, this ever-present truth is available to us in each instant. Calming the turbulence of our mind and body to realize and embody it is the practice of our lives.

For now perhaps let's just be with this gradual disintegration of the self we thought we once knew. The self of our wants and needs, our hardships, our worries and regrets, bitterness and despair, even our hopes and dreams. These features are all present and valid, yes, but they are not the whole story. Abandoning our idea of a self comprised of these empty, temporary things is the pivotal step off the path we have tread, away from the endless struggle for satisfaction, and into the perfect peace of liberation and joy.

Maybe someday we can greet each other, shake hands,

and share a grin about who is actually meeting there. We have no idea! As far as we can tell, it's no one at all: just two arrows colliding in midair and then falling down, laughing. This is how we might come forth when we've abandoned the ego self and realized that we simply *are*. It's how we might behave in the world of traffic lights and coworkers and to-dos, which is the path we have been discovering together all along. It starts with mindful, openhearted awareness of what is, without the filter of the ego self. It includes work and play, love and compassion, mistakes and forgiveness. It is beautiful and sad, poignant and precious, ephemeral and infinite. It is us.

REFLECTION: One Last Look

Return now to what you wrote about the constituent parts of yourself. This is not an exercise in linguistics or a philosophical parlor trick. Rather, it is about the resolution of your suffering and the liberation of your life. It is about finding ease and clarity amid all those turbulent waves. It's about making that appointment with your life that Thich Nhat Hanh talked about. The appointment that is always right here waiting for you to show up.

So take a good look and examine each of these elements. Trace their features, their shapes and movements, and their many pieces, past and present. Consider the material and the immaterial, the obvious and the subtle. Peering into their multifaceted and impermanent identities, discover again their emptiness. Just be very still and look very closely. Is anything left?

MEDITATION: Vigil for Your Self

Please sit comfortably, taking up a posture that is gentle and alert. You have come a long way to be here. Perhaps take a moment to honor the journey you have taken.

Be with your body. Feel its sensations. Just noticing and being, right here, right now.

Welcome to your seat under the bodhi tree. Visualize a bed of soft grasses under you. Imagine the leaves and branches gently swaying in the breeze overhead. Feel yourself here. Twenty-five hundred years ago, someone else was sitting right here. We call them Buddha. Now it is your turn. It is always your turn.

Now you sit the night's watch, the vigil for your self.

Having examined several techniques and methods to awaken your loving heart, you are now invited to turn and face yourself, this person for whom you have so much care and concern. The one who experiences your joys and sorrows, successes and mistakes.

Starting from the outside, take a moment to traverse your skin. Scan it patiently with your mind's eye. Feel into its many stretches and curves. Notice any hair on your skin and any other parts and features of your body. Your eyes. Your ears. Your hands and feet. Your belly moving with the breath. See it all here.

Taking a step deeper, acknowledge your muscles, bones, and sinews. The flesh and blood that build you, the engines that carry you throughout your day and rest with you at night. Sense into your many organs: your heart beating, your lungs expanding and receding, your stomach churning. Recognize the many others, seen and unseen, felt and unfelt. You are invited to honor them now.

Now consider, underneath and intertwined, the many nerves and sense receptors of your body. An unimaginable network of wiring along which innumerable electric impulses ride, carrying the signals of your life experience. Imagine how this web of sensations and perceptions travel around your body, up your spine, and into your brain.

Imagine, if you can, this home of your mind, its soft tissue and moist curves, its mysterious layers, corners and epicenters, its miraculous blend of neurons and synapses. This is a place we never see, we never encounter, we never feel. And it is a place with which we are so very deeply familiar.

Now we can acknowledge our thoughts. These ideas and visions and memories arising in this moment. We may discover that we cannot trace their origin, nor can we pinpoint the moment they disappear. Yet we see them here now. Always arising anew.

Still occupying this space in your mind, you are invited now to turn to your past. In the legend of the Buddha's awakening, it is said that he examined his past lives. Take a moment now to revisit the time of your birth. Imagine the context, what it might have looked and felt like for you. Moving on, briefly scan your history, seeing yourself as an infant, a toddler, a child, a young person, and on, and all the many experiences that happened along the way. See as well the many roles you have played. Perhaps it's son or daughter, student, employee, partner, friend, athlete, and many others. Spot yourself in these different phases of your life, and offer yourself a deep bow.

Perhaps acknowledge, as you review your past, the many changes that have unfolded. Changes in place and time.

Changes in relationships. Changes in your physical body, both the obvious ones and the ever-changingness of everything that comprises it. Acknowledge the breath and nutrients that have come and gone, the innumerable cells that have birthed and died, the atoms that have spun their wild orbits and passed through. Where did these many pieces come from, and where have they gone?

Look back further still. Stretch your mind into the time before your birth. There were two people, each bringing with them the entirety of their own experience, their own physical and mental ways of being. Beyond them, there were thousands of ancestors and, further still, your numerous evolutionary predecessors, all the way back to cells dividing just as they did in the primordial oceans billions of years ago. Just try to imagine all these incredible journeys.

These are your past lives. You are the Buddha, and you can see them all, right now. Go ahead, remember your past lives.

Now turn your gaze to the lives ahead. These swirling conditions, components, and ideas of you, here they are all now. Where will they go next? Imagine your body and mind as they gradually shed these numerous tiny elements. They will not be here forever. Watch them gently fade, pass through, spin off into their own unknowable paths. The lens of you can open up to this vast future ahead, all its infinite possibilities, the experience of which we can only pretend to fathom. These are your future lives. This is the body of the future Buddha.

Gently steer your traveling mind back to your place here in your seat. Now, quickly, tell me, who are you? Which part of this epic journey is what makes you you? If you don't find an answer, wonderful. Be with that. If you do, beautiful. Say that thing to yourself. Examine it carefully. Where did it come from? What is it made of? How soon will it change? What separates it from the numerous other aspects of you? Is that really you? *All* of you?

Here arises a new breath. You are invited to immerse yourself in it fully. Yes, you are home. The bodhi tree is offering you its loving shade. Gently lift your eyes. What do you see? A speck on the wall, a glimmer in the window, a shadow on the floor? After sitting his own vigil for the night, the Buddha looked up and saw the morning star. It echoed back what, deep in his heart, he already knew. The truth of him and of all beings was perfectly clear and unblemished in that instant. This is your instant. Whatever is before you now is your morning star. Hear what it has to say. Let it into your heart.

"Wonder of wonders," the Buddha proclaimed.

Wonder of wonders.

✦

That's enough fingers pointing at the moon for now. Now it's your turn to be the moon.

Chapter 10

Walking the Empty Path

Still, there are times I am bewildered by each mile I have traveled,
each meal I have eaten, each person I have known,
each room in which I have slept. As ordinary as it all appears,
there are times when it is beyond my imagination.

— JHUMPA LAHIRI, *Interpreter of Maladies*

I travel on the great... Way.
The arrow is out.
There are no obsessions in my mind.
Having gone into the empty house,
I rejoice.

— SUBHA, in *First Buddhist Women*, ed. SUSAN MURCOTT

My knee is propped up on the steering wheel of my car as my thumbs tap out a response to a pointed Google review. I'm merging onto the highway on my way home from Awake. It's late for me, about 11:30 p.m., and the dark Denver night is cut by the rush of taillights speeding past. Just a few weeks ago, I had crushed the front right quarter of my car by mindlessly backing out of my parking garage spot, forgetting that there was a two-foot square pillar immediately to my right.

I look up from my phone to see that my car is straddling the bright yellow line between my lane and the shoulder, which is outlined by a low concrete barrier between it and the steep gravel hill on the other side. I wake up to that instant with an abruptly casual thought: "I could die now." The next thought loafs behind it, subtle and strange: "That would be okay."

It was summer 2022, and my obsession with my alcohol-free bar endeavor had approached a precipice. The whirlwind of inventories, maintenance, vendors, planning, AV snafus, plumbing disasters, and the daily deluge of this chaotic business had worn down my psyche. Most withering of all were the relationships: the rushed and impersonal hiring, the obsolete welcome and training, the cycles of dedication and neglect (theirs, mine, ours), the soft fading departures and the staccato, bitter exits. Having intended to create a place of personal connection and peace, I had succumbed to othering the staff and the place we were all trying to build. Despite the generous public adoration, my experience of Awake at that point had become grotesque, polluting all realms of my life experience and, perhaps, most of all, my family.

I quit drinking alcohol at the beginning of a global movement that was normalizing abstinence, coupled with an exponential flood of next-generation nonalcoholic beverages. Rather than fully embracing the magical lessening of this decision, I opted instead to fill it by creating and launching this new bar concept in Denver. It was a classic case of believing I had to do more in order to be the best version of me.

I didn't just launch the bar, mind you. After just a few months of initial success, I proceeded to invest time and resources into building a robust franchising program, with sophisticated operating manuals, multistate franchise filings, and a steady pipeline of interested entrepreneurs. I was doing all this while upholding my day job as the leader of a health policy consulting firm. The evidence is clear: When we think we need more to be fulfilled, nothing we seek will ever satisfy us.

That brief moment of mortally ambivalent despair in my car that night scared me. Fortunately, it turned out to be the shock that my system needed to seek a different direction. Within a few weeks of that night, I closed Awake and gradually shed my attachment to that dream. It took a few months, but eventually, in a ceremony of its own, I delivered the remaining assets to a local charity and then, finally, the remnants to a garbage dump. The beautiful rectangular Awake sign that hung over our door, Zen-like in its deep black background and clear golden lettering, is by now covered with new layers of refuse.

It was fascinating how palpably my body-mind changed as soon as the doors to Awake closed. Almost instantly, I was sleeping better, feeling happier, and reacquainting myself with gratitude for each precious day. Rather than waking up to the anxiety of the numerous open ends I would fail to tie up, I felt freer to greet what the day might bring. By leaving Awake behind, I was finally able to be the person that it called me to be.

Despite all the hardship it created for me and the ostensible failure that it was in traditional financial terms, I do not regret the time I dedicated to Awake for an instant. I met so many incredible people, including the staff, the guests, the vendors, and the hundreds of supporters who lent me their kind encouragement. Even more so, I honor it as an ingredient of my past life that led to my present one. We can acknowledge our many hardships, errors, and pain, but in terms of the choices we have made, each one has delivered us to where we are now. The past is perfectly designed to produce the present. So I have adopted the path of not quibbling with the past. We can never know where the alternative courses may have led us, but perhaps we can trust that the one we are on is the one for us. There is no path other than the step we are taking right now into the next moment.

The month after I closed Awake, I was meditating one morning and the fall sun crept through my closet window, spreading its soft singe across my face. What I realized in that moment had been whispering to me for many years, but only then did it become clear in a way that has not faltered since. I knew that there was one true thing I needed to know, and it was the only thing I ever really needed to say. It's what I told you at the very beginning of our journey: *There is absolutely nothing wrong with us. Whatever our circumstances, whatever our difficulties and needs, traumas and mistakes, we are, at the same time, not lacking a single thing. Whatever we have gone through and whatever is to come, we have always been whole and complete from the very beginning and we will be so forever.*

That morning, I sat down and started to write this book.

The Promise of Emptiness

So we embrace the obvious question: What does this mean for our real life, right here and now? What is the difference between awakening to this realization of our own perfection and forgetting it? That tree is still a tree. This desk is still a desk. And our relationships may still be in need of some attention.

The answer: We can acknowledge all these things, all these multiplicities that shine forth as the world around us, the milieu of our lives. Rather than seeing them as separate, though — which invariably inspires unfulfillable craving for the things we desire and unavoidable fear of those we reject — we maintain our mindful, compassionate awareness of their underlying emptiness and unity. With this clarity, we can stop clinging to impermanent things, we can stop chasing illusions. We are free to live in the unmistakable eternal beauty of the moment before us, right in the midst of the messy reality of our daily lives. This is not about the perfect moment on the perfect hillside in perfect lighting, with the perfect latte, wine, friend, or lover. It's about wherever we may be right now, and appreciating that it is enough.

Having lived in the quest for more and the faith that it will fulfill us, we can now see that it is by distilling our lives, by lessening our ideas of *should*, that our true nature and that of all beings can shine forth. It's the only place where true peace and fulfillment can be found. How do we respond to the next moment, then? We can trust our next steps on our path. Everything is, in a way, exactly the same. And, unmistakably, every single thing has changed. Having traced the origins of this moment back to their "source in vastness and pure presence," as poet Danna Faulds wrote, you can "emerge so new, so fresh, that you don't know who you are." That's the perfect place to take a breath and start again.

REFLECTION: Where Have You Arrived?

Recall the intentions you established when you started reading this book. Pausing for a quiet moment, consider the ways in which those intentions have arisen for you during this journey. We commenced with an exploration of your being in the world, with time, space, and your own thoughts as vital touchpoints of this experience. Drawing on those teachings and mindfulness practices, we entered into the practical realities of your life: work, play, and relationships. Nearing the end, we turned toward transcendence, led by inquiry into your self.

A student once asked his spiritual teacher, "What have you personally gained from meditating over the years?"

The teacher responded, "To be honest, I haven't gained that much. But I can tell you a lot about what I have lost."

Consider, perhaps, what you have gained on this journey. Then turn toward what you may have left behind. How have you lessened your life, your self, your mind, and your heart? Now, breathing gently, see how you answer the question: Where are you now?

Enlightenment Itself Is Empty

Of all the spiritual ideas, enlightenment can be among the most problematic. On the one hand, popular culture has "mored" this concept, considering it a mythological state in which the regular, physical person might levitate or vanish into thin air, having somehow earned a ticket to a magical paradise. On the other, it expresses a final and permanent quality, a state of being that, once attained, can never be rescinded or forgotten.

While some expressions of enlightenment in classical forms of Buddhism may sound like this, inquiry into the nature of enlightenment might reveal something quite different and much more ordinary. Recall the two cornerstones of emptiness that we have explored: impermanence and no-self. Everything is always changing, over the course of its lifetime and in each new moment. Also, all things lack an inherent identity to call its own that isn't contingent on an infinite array of other, temporary causes and conditions. These two facets of all experience also apply to enlightenment. So, as with everything else, let's not get too attached to it.

At the same time, enlightenment offers us inspiration to turn toward our present lives. A common Buddhist term for the experience of enlightenment is *paramita*, which means "one who has arrived at the other shore." As we cultivate our ability to awaken to our own emptiness and that of all things, softening our attachments to our ideas, judgments, and preconceived notions and freeing ourselves to enter into the next moment with a clear, unencumbered mind and heart, we may discover that we are on that "other shore." That shore is still just exactly where we are — in the car, at the grocery store, or lying in bed — but everything has changed. We might also realize that we have in fact been on that shore all along; it's just that we have now looked up to see.

Thus continues the beautiful, mysterious dance between the relative aspects of our experience and the absolute ones, the multiplicity and the unity, the radiant details and the translucent inner core. Both are always true, and so enlightenment is always present, even as it ebbs and flows alongside the ever-evolving experience of our lives. True freedom arises when we let this 360-degree perspective fully enter and permeate our hearts. Pleasure and pain and our attachment to them will continually arise, as will our opportunity to experience them wholeheartedly and then let them pass through. This invitation is not hidden on a distant hillside in Tibet or the prize awarded after a long, tempestuous journey. It's right here, awaiting your answer right now.

You may doubt that this can be true. You may buy into the notion, as we all so often do, that there is so much more you need to do to prepare for such a moment. There must be a lot more time and effort and sacrifice needed in order to attain the peace you seek, right? After all your exhausting efforts, how could it be so simple? This is how we've been trained to think of every aspect of our lives. There must be groundwork and classes and clever words and the right outfit. Maybe you haven't even brushed your teeth yet! I am honored to be the one to tell you that not one of those things, as enjoyable and meaningful as they may be, is going to prepare you for enlightenment. If we think of these things that way, all they are is obstacles. Your enlightenment is already here, contained in this moment, however it is, whatever it looks like. And, just like the Buddha, you are perfectly worthy of it.

In a famous Zen koan, an aspiring student, Chao-chou, asked the master Nan-chuan, "What is the Way?"

Nan-chuan answered, "Ordinary mind is the Way."

Enlightenment is not fancy or esoteric. It is not a riddle for your inner Pooh Bear to "think, think, think" its way to. It does not require denial of your values, abandonment of your loved ones, or retreat from your day-to-day responsibilities.

It is just the natural state of your being as it traverses your precious life. Congratulations.

The Radical Art of Walking the Empty Path

Here it comes again, the ever-present question: What do I do now? In this section we'll revisit and adapt practical tools and simple reminders for walking this empty path in your daily life. In each, you will find the fundamental intention of lessening, peeling back the layers of all the ideas and judgments we add to our moments that only serve to cloud our awareness of our truest nature and underlying peace.

As we know by now, this can happen right here, in an instant. At the same time, this is a lifelong practice. We've spent eons more-ing; those habits are deeply ingrained. Believing that the relative aspects of life — this side and that, good and bad, near and far — are the only true life, we've created illusions and attachments that have cooed us into what Tara Brach calls the "trance of imperfection," the belief that we are not enough and never can be. From now on, with each step on the path, we might acknowledge and release these habit energies to awaken to our inherent, abiding sufficiency. Here are ten steps to get you started on your journey.

1. Breathing

It's foolishly simple. Your breath is your honored companion through your life. It contains winds of the ancient past and the fresh breeze of the present. It will always be there to help you remember your truest intentions. Having practiced concentration on the breath during meditation, you can now reference it at any moment to suspend and soften your swirling thoughts and attachments. Maybe you can discover if anything else there is worthy of your attention. Let your breath fill your belly and ease your posture. Welcome its calm. It's difficult to be angry when we're mindful of our breathing. It's almost impossible to yell. Our instinct to react gives way to our intention to respond.

2. Embodiment

How is your body doing in this moment? Listen to it. Incapable of thinking and yet deeply knowing, our bodies are a gateway to authentically experiencing our lives. Stay harmonized with it as you navigate your day, and it will help you return to presence. If you are feeling especially confused in your thoughts, try shifting your attention all the way down to your feet. Ask yourself, "What do my feet have to say about this?" Meanwhile, you are pausing and softening.

Whether in a dedicated format like tapping or doing a body scan, or, in brief moments, sensing into your stomach as you drive your car, I invite you to embody your experience of life. Whatever we perceive to be its flaws, our body is our only vehicle for navigating our days and awakening to our deepest truth.

3. Questioning Thoughts

"Thought after thought arises in mind," the Kannon Sutra echoes. And, it continues, "thought after thought is not separate from mind." Thoughts are not separate from us. They are not our enemy. And yet we so often let them preoccupy, delude, and deceive us. To transform our lifelong habits, we might experiment with a healthy skepticism of our thoughts. Instead of reflexively believing and following them, we can soften our attachment to their dictates and expand the boundaries of our freedom.

If we find ourselves caught in cycling thoughts, the simplest version of this practice can be a brief: "Is this true?" As we have practiced, the question can also include "Am I so sure?" "How does this thought serve me and others?" "What would my life be like if I set this thought aside for just a moment?" With this simple interruption of our "mind road," we haven't stopped thinking, but we have reclaimed the wheel to set a fresh course.

4. Naming Emotions

"Name it to tame it," author Brené Brown says. As with thoughts, there is nothing inherently wrong with our emotions. They can be our teachers, gateways to expanding our capacity to be with what is. They can also be a source of deep, painful suffering. Whatever our emotions may be in any situation, we can honor them as valid. By identifying them, we can draw a line between them and our intentions, integrity, and responsibility for our next step.

The appropriate response to tragedy is often grief, and only we can know the appropriate length of time that we should spend watering that particular garden. If we suspect we have lost our center, though, having compromised our intentions by attaching to an emotion that no longer serves us, the most effective tool may be to simply acknowledge the presence of that emotion by naming it, perhaps out loud. This can have the effect of sharpening our awareness of it, thereby softening its control over us. We might recognize that, while it is not separate from us, it is not us, certainly not all of us. It is a part of our experience and, like all parts of our experience, it will eventually pass through.

5. Attuning to Emptiness

You know the drill by now, friends. Take any feature of your life: an object that you crave, a person you can't stand, an idea you are fascinated by, or a memory or fantasy that is distracting you. Examine it closely and carefully, observing as many of its features as you can. What are its attributes? Where did it come from? What conditions were necessary for it to arise? How long will it last? How might it be changing, right now? Which of these features makes it what it is? In other words, what defines it as the thing you believe it to be? Having explored each of these questions, what's left? How is it separate from you?

Even as that thing is blue and round and sitting on the table across the room, it is also empty. You might still go pick it up, but perhaps you'll do so with a lighter heart and a freer mind.

6. Softening the Other

We have explored a number of techniques for softening our othering, the opinions, assumptions, and ideas we have about people, which can block our view of their truer nature. If we can look more deeply, we may discover the aspect of them that is empty and thus undifferentiated from us. The

Softening Our Stories meditation in chapter 6 is a thorough exploration of this possibility.

Strategies for remembering the truest nature of those around us include reimagining that person as a newborn baby, as yet unblemished by life experience and whatever difficulties may have arisen between you and them. Similarly, you might recall the allegory of the empty canoe in chapter 6, where our attachment to blame and resentment can soften if we remember that others we encounter, like us, are impermanent and lacking self-nature.

I had a direct experience of this recently. I was in the Phoenix area riding in an Uber with my family when we saw a car ahead of us with odd spinning cones on its top and sides. It was going slower than the flow of traffic and I started to imagine who might be driving it that would fit the assumptions and stereotypes that I still, alas, maintain about people who might drive that way. As we pulled closer, I peered into the driver's seat to discover that *there was no one there*. It was a self-driving car, the first one I had seen in person. I had a nice chuckle with my family as we considered all the scenarios in which we might get angry at the driver of this car, only to discover there isn't one. I wonder how many people are carrying around a grudge against the driver of a car who does not exist. How many more of us are carrying around anger at others that has nothing to do with who they really are?

7. Defining Responsibility

Even if we can remember the emptiness we share with all beings, we can still acknowledge our unique diversity, our beautiful differences, and the not-so-beautiful harms and offenses that others perpetrate against us. Relationships are complicated and can be difficult, even with those we love and cherish. Embodying compassion does not mean we ignore these important aspects of our lives or their impact on us. We still get to draw boundaries and, to fully realize our inherent freedom, we must. Freedom and responsibility are two sides of the same coin.

Whether at a time of reflection about a relationship issue or perhaps in the heat of the moment, a helpful practice can be to simply ask, "What is my responsibility here?" In doing so, we remember that there are boundaries to our realms of influence. We also invite ourselves to focus more clearly on those things we can control, starting with our own mind and body. Then we get to choose what our next word will be or decide whose company we keep. As we soften our attachment to how we think others should be, we immerse ourselves ever deeper into the true heart of compassion, strengthening our boundaries and integrity with our bona fide responsibilities.

8. Maintaining Forgiveness

Of all these steps on the empty path I am offering you, forgiveness can be the most difficult. Recalling both our heartfelt compassion and our sturdiest boundaries, we can choose when the spirit of forgiveness is ripe. Acknowledging and then perhaps wading through our attachments to how others may respond, and whether or not we believe they deserve it, we can practice the process of forgiveness when we are ready to be at peace with the situation. It may take a while.

So too is the case with us. The fruit of self-forgiveness is ripe once we see that the regret we carry is not serving us or others. While some degree of remorse, repair, or other action toward resolution may be warranted, we can keep asking these questions each time the pang of shame returns: How is it serving us? To whom do we owe this suffering?

As we let our thoughts settle, we can inquire into whether our ongoing self-punishment and belief in our tragic flaws may be fueling cycles of behavior that produce results similar to those we regret. I encourage you to find opportunities for deep, focused attention to these ceremonies of grace, and I also invite you to remember the essence of these practices with a simple "I am forgiven" or, toward another, "I forgive you now." Even if you don't wholly believe it at the time, uttering these words can help soften your heart and awaken your love.

9. Asking Your Self

The heart of the "beast," the holiest of holies, the innermost of the sanctums of emptiness is your very own self. It is both the root cause and the only true liberator of your suffering. In any situation, however pivotal or trivial, you can invite the question, "Who am I?" as a tool for turning away from the dualism of self and other and toward the wholeness of emptiness. Who is experiencing this discomfort? Who is angry right now? Who is going to be on that stage next week? If you answer such questions wholeheartedly, then every place is your true home, every experience is a timeless teacher, and every instant is a miraculous encounter with an unknowable and abiding truth — a flash of lightning in a summer cloud.

10. ARIA

Several teachings are available to give you both a fast-acting tactic for pausing in a difficult situation to explore your attitudes and some best next steps to take in a more methodical way. In the Mindfulness-Based Stress Reduction course I took, we learned the STOP approach (Stop, Take a breath, Observe, Proceed). Tara Brach is a well-known teacher of the RAIN technique (Recognize, Allow, Investigate, Nurture). Taking what I have learned from these practices and others, while refining them to more closely align with the spirit of emptiness that I am conveying here, I offer you the ARIA technique: Acknowledge, Rest, Inquire, Advance.

Acknowledge: This is the simple act of awareness, noticing what is present in the situation before the instinct to judge and analyze arises. I selected this term because it does not connote any inkling of agreement with what may have happened; it's a way of seeing that explicitly intends to remain neutral. As we acknowledge, we can do our best to witness all aspects of the situation as we directly experienced it.

Rest: This is the important pause. It is the space between reactivity, where we are driven by our habit energies, and responding, where we arouse our truer intentions. With rest we give ourselves the opportunity to linger for an extra beat in our kind awareness of what is happening, to let the energies settle and allow our truer selves to come forth.

Inquire: In our spirit of nonjudging curiosity, in this step we sharpen our gaze at the situation to identify what deeper truths it may have to offer. This may involve questioning some of our impulsive judgments so we can soften our attachment to them. Meanwhile, we attune to our underlying emotions to identify what most needs our tender care and attention. What is at the heart of the matter? That is what we are seeking to understand.

Advance: Having afforded ourselves rest and inquiry, we can now consider what the best next step for us is. This ARIA practice is not about cloistering ourselves in a hut. It is about how we come forth in the world, which we get to choose. Having sung our ARIA, we might have more confidence that our choice aligns with our truest nature.

REFLECTION: A Day in the Life on the Empty Path

We are approaching the end of our journey together. We know that the next moment is coming soon. With all that we have explored and practiced, it may be helpful to visualize what your life can be like as you follow the empty path.

As you know, your circumstances are still your circumstances. You will probably wake up in the same bed as before, wear clothes from the same closet, and eat food from the same pantry. At least for a while, the other activities of your day will likely mirror those that came before. Similarly, your memories, regrets, and dreams are all still present, as are your relationships, both the easier and more difficult ones. What has changed?

You might find that you are more aware of your breath and other bodily sensations and that, perhaps, they afford you a broader awareness of how you are experiencing the moments of your day. You might be more attuned to your experience as both a witness and a participant. Ever so gradually, you might discover that your thoughts and judgments, while still bustling, have softened. At times, rather than a torrent, they might be a gently flowing stream, one you can choose to dip into or not.

In your work as well as in your hobbies, you might find moments where the steady march of goals and deadlines and demands starts to wander off the beaten path, if just for a little while. You might notice the underlying story that the brief hallway conversation offers you, or the radiant nature of something as mundane as your cell phone case, or the awe-inspiring complexity, history, and aliveness of that otherwise boring meeting. Perhaps you will find new seeds of meaning and fulfillment in your endeavors and, as you water them, they may grow until you find yourself in an entirely new environment, whether or not it's in the same place.

Your experience of your relationships may soften as well. You might find yourself listening a bit longer before you speak. You might catch yourself invested in understanding a bit more and reacting a bit less. Maybe you celebrate a small victory of abandoning the impulse to fire off a terse email. You might also find yourself more interested in establishing and maintaining your boundaries in these relationships, inquiring where the best place is to offer your love and compassion.

Perhaps, as much as anything else, that tormenting voice of your inner critic might start to soften. Your regrets, shame, and self-doubt will likely stay with you, but your relationship to them can change. No longer identifying them as *you*, you might start to see some space between your life and those harsh judgments. You begin to recognize their themes and have newfound freedom to inquire into them more deeply.

Underneath them, you might discover what is true, has always been true, of you.

However your path unfolds, whatever new joys and hardships may arise, you can trust in the intention to experience them as fully and honestly as you can. Setting aside all the unnecessary things — the overlay of preconceived ideas, expectations, and judgments — you can practice the art of lessening. You might live in faith that, whatever happens, your empty, undefiled nature is always worthy of peace and fulfillment. You *are* peace and fulfillment themselves, just waiting to shine forth.

MEDITATION: Singing Your ARIA

Welcome to your timeless home. Welcome to your one true place. Perhaps let yourself surrender to your seat and to this moment. Acknowledging all that surrounds you, settle in to all that you are.

Feel your breath as it fills your body, heart, and mind and then passes through. Embrace its gentle path, its beckoning to peace.

Just sit and rest with your kind awareness for a few moments. You belong here.

Consider what barrier to peace may be arising for you now. Is it a recent incident, an ongoing conflict, an ancient regret? Maybe it is an opinion of yourself or another. Maybe it is something quite simple, a modest mistake you made in thought, speech, or action this morning. Whatever it is can be an opportunity for awakening. Find that one thing for you now and settle into your remembering of it.

We begin by *acknowledging* this thing in your life for all

that it is. What does the situation or idea look like? What people and places might be involved? What words are spoken? What do you witness to be the impact on or the reaction of others? All these things are here now. As best as you can, pause your instinct to judge them as positive or negative, to be maintained or rejected, and try to see them just as they are. What happened?

Take your time to be here in the spirit of openhearted acknowledgment. See what is to be seen and hear what is to be heard. Feel what is to be felt. If pain or sadness or regret or shame arises, be compassionate and nurturing to yourself as you honor it. As you continue to breathe, allow yourself an embodiment of comfort by placing a hand on your heart. Perhaps whisper to yourself, "It's okay. There can be space for this."

Now we pause in this place and allow a syllable of *rest.* In your awareness of this obstacle and all that it means for you and others, here is a moment of being with it. This is where the quarter and half notes of your acknowledgment turn to rest notes, a silent pause as the melody still rings. Your breath is your companion through this space. Listen to it as you hold in your awareness all that this challenging experience is for you.

Arousing now your curious beginner's mind, perhaps reapproach this circumstance with *inquiry:* How does acknowledgment of this situation feel in your body right now? Is there ease or tension? How does it sit in your stomach or chest? How does it resonate in your jaw or brow?

What are the causes and conditions of this situation, for you or others, or the places where it may have occurred?

Scan the history of these pieces as you imagine them. What are their many varying contexts? From where did they arise? Understanding perhaps that you cannot fully know these answers, just explore these possibilities for a moment.

Turning to the thoughts you have about this situation, the opinions and analysis, the gaps you have filled with your own assumptions and conclusions, are you certain they are true? Are you obligated to believe them? What would your life be like if you didn't believe them 100 percent? Again, you are invited to let the questions linger, abiding in that space before answers rush in.

Looking deeper to your own underlying emotions — perhaps fear, longing, shame, or grief — which one stands out as in most need of your tender care right now? This may be a feeling you have carried with you for a long time. Look to yourself now and to the versions of you that may have experienced this feeling so many times before. Send each of them the love and compassion you find available to you. If finding that is difficult, you might still utter softly, "I see you." "I care about you."

Now, gathering your courage, your inherent enoughness, consider what the best way to *advance* in this situation might be. Are there words yet to be said, actions yet to be taken? Are there new extensions of care to you or to others that are still calling to you? What does it look like to approach these actions with an open and loving heart?

With all that you are, all the tender love and concern that you have, how do you advance into the next moment? Where does your next foot fall on your path to reconciling your beautiful, abundant self with this difficulty in your life?

Whatever the causes and impacts of this situation have been, what will be the causes and impacts of your next step?

Now you are invited to breathe into this new moment, taking note of how you feel in your body and of any new resolve that may be arising in your mind. Everything about this situation, all that it has been, is now gone. At the same time, you are a new edition of you. Welcome to your new life. It begins now. What will you create?

✦

As you proceed into your day and those to come, keep this practice with you. Even in a brief instant, maybe a few breaths longer than usual, you can:

Acknowledge your situation, in all its innumerable components.

Rest in that space of openhearted awareness.

Inquire into its deepest truths.

Advance into the next moment of your new life, with an intention to generate the most appropriate, loving response.

Sing your ARIA. Fill your heart. Lend your hand. Share your voice.

Everything that you have ever been, all that you will ever be, the infinite sources of your being that comprise and affirm you — all of it is arising here, now. You have always been walking the empty path, and you always will be. Don't look around for it. You are already there.

Acknowledgments

While I dedicate this book to my precious children, I wrote it because of my wife, Christy. Your initial intention to write a book is what reignited my dream to do the same. More importantly, it is your loving support, incisive wisdom, and earthy, elegant manner of being in the world that cocreate our life together. This book could only grow out of our shared soil.

I also owe homage and gratitude to my dear mother. As the selfless giving tree that incubated me through my tumultuous childhood and beyond, you taught me how to love. It is impossible to fathom where I would be without you — certainly not here.

And to my father, a writer, thinker, and practitioner of contemplative prayer, akin to meditation: you taught me perseverance in the face of adversity and that love can abide in any circumstance.

I would be remiss if I didn't acknowledge Marjorie Pardue, my fourth-grade teacher and the first to convey to me that I might have something unique to offer the world. The confidence you instilled in me carried me through many dark places and fed inspiration into this book. I am also indebted to Pat Hume, my high school English teacher who taught me to write. You interrupted my careening life to persuade me there might be something more tender and compassionate lying dormant beneath. And to another teacher, Professor Darryl Caterine: your course on postmodernism and the American Dream was the defining intellectual experience of my life. Your comments and encouragement on my papers penetrated my hazy college facade to remind me that I mattered.

I am guided along the Zen way by my dear teacher and friend, Peggy Metta Sheehan Roshi, who demonstrates clarity, wisdom, and compassion in her heartfelt practice and daily life. The fortuitous crossing of my path with you and the Zen Center of Denver is an unknowable gift. I likewise extend my love and gratitude to the other teachers at the Zen Center and my dharma brothers and sisters there with whom I share many tender, quiet moments. Thank you for your wisdom, example, and never-failing help.

I want to thank my dear lifelong friends, including my brother. You continue to prop me up through difficulty and teach me the virtue of absurdity and ease. Our wide-ranging conversations have informed several aspects of this book. You know who you are. May you know how grateful and fulfilled I am to call you my friend.

There are three people who, triple-handedly, are the only reason this book is in your hands. The first is my inimitable book-writing coach, Bess Matassa. I came to you with an amateurish boil of vague ideas, and you extracted from me the coherent concept that became these pages. As my first true editor, you patiently and kindly steered through my ego resistance and taught me the peace of trusting collaboration.

The second is my agent, Leslie Meredith at Dystel, Goderich & Bourret. Among my many rejectors, you were the one who saw me and the potential beauty of this work. You were also essential to translating my ideas and practices to reach readers in their place, where they are.

The third is my editor, Jason Gardner, and your colleagues at New World Library. You have my enduring gratitude for taking a chance on this rookie author. I can only assume we share a conviction that ideas and practices rooted in love and vulnerability still have the power to transform lives.

Notes

Introduction

p. 1   References to the Heart Sutra are adapted from the Zen Center of Denver chant booklet.

Chapter 1: Reclaiming Time

p. 25   References to Master Hakuin's *Song of Zazen* are adapted from the Zen Center of Denver chant booklet.

p. 27   *"you have an appointment with your life"*: Thich Nhat Hanh, https://youtu.be/6V2lEtKy7rY

p. 36   *"Life is like getting on a small boat"*: Shunryu Suzuki, *Zen Is Right Now.* (Boulder: Shambhala, 2021), 93.

p. 38   *"It's passing and it's precious"*: Tara Brach, "The Reality of Change: Embracing This Living Dying World," live talk, May 24, 2017, available at https://www.tarabrach.com/reality-change.

p. 40   *"Out beyond ideas of wrongdoing and rightdoing"*: Jelaluddin Rumi, "A Great Wagon," in *The Essential Rumi*, trans. Coleman Barks with John Moyne (San Francisco: HarperSanFransisco, 1995).

Chapter 3: Getting to Know Your Mind

p. 88   *"Ten thousand flowers in spring"*: Wu-Men, *The Gateless Barrier: The Wu-Men Kuan*, trans. Robert Aitken (Berkeley, CA: North Point, 1991).

Chapter 5: Discovering the True Joy of Play

p. 119   *"I learned that being awake can be as flavor-specific as dreaming"*: Mike Gordon, *Doniac Schvice Newsletter*, Late Fall 1995, https://phishby theyears.wordpress.com/wp-content/uploads/2018/09/1995-5-late -fall.pdf.

p. 128   *"benefits in turning toward discomfort"*: J. David Creswell, "Learning to Accept Discomfort Could Help You Thrive," *Scientific American*, November 10, 2023, https://www.scientificamerican.com/article/learning -to-accept-discomfort-could-help-you-thrive.

p. 128   *"found that people who can face"*: Emily C. Willroth et al., "Judging Emotions as Good or Bad: Individual Differences and Associations with Psychological Health," *Emotion* 23, no. 7 (October 2023): 1876– 90, https://pubmed.ncbi.nlm.nih.gov/36913276.

p. 130   *"I had to have my attachments broken"*: Julia Butterfly Hill, "Julia in the Storm," December 23, 2010, https://www.youtube.com/watch ?v=8tsvJ1XaXvo.

Chapter 6: Coming Forth in Compassion

p. 156   *"all spiritual traditions"*: Sebene Selassie, *You Belong: A Call for Connection* (San Francisco: HarperOne, 2020), 40.

p. 157   *"are used to carry out oppression"*: Sebene Selassie, *You Belong: A Call for Connection* (San Francisco: HarperOne, 2020), 43.

Chapter 7: Being the Love You Are

p. 182   *"both speaker and listener"*: Thich Nhat Hanh, *The Heart of the Buddha's Teaching* (New York: Harmony Books, 2015), 87.

Chapter 9: Abandoning the Ego Self

p. 223   *"To study the Buddha Way is to study the self"*: Eihei Dogen, "Actualizing the Fundamental Point: Genjo Koan," in *Moon in a Dewdrop: Writings of Zen Master Dogen*, ed. Kazuaki Tanahashi (New York: North Point, 1985), 70.

Chapter 10: Walking the Empty Path

p. 241   *Having traced the origins of this moment*: Danna Faulds, "Trusting Prana," *Emmanuelle* (blog), https://mindfulness.emmanuelle-dalpra .com/trusting-prana-by-danna-faulds.

About the Author

Billy Wynne has studied Buddhism and mindfulness for thirty years. He received lay Zen Buddhist ordination from the Zen Center of Denver, where he now teaches classes and serves on the board. He is also a certified meditation teacher in the Insight tradition under Jack Kornfield and Tara Brach.

After traveling the world with an NGO that provides medical care to children, Billy launched a career as a health and well-being entrepreneur. He founded and serves as chairman of Impact Health, a consultancy serving large healthcare organizations including Cleveland Clinic, Fortune 500 companies, and charitable foundations. In 2020 Billy founded one of the world's first alcohol-free bars, Awake. Frequently quoted by national news outlets, including *The New York Times* and *The Washington Post*, he now provides mindfulness-based coaching to mission-driven executives.

In addition to the Zen Center of Denver, Billy has served on the boards of Operation Smile, Health365, and Cherish Children Adoption International. In 2023 he was appointed by Governor Jared Polis to serve on Colorado's Natural

Medicine Advisory Board, which is implementing the state's new psychedelic therapy program.

Billy received a BA from Dartmouth College and a law degree from the University of Virginia. For fun he plays keyboard in two improvisational rock bands. He lives just outside Denver with his wife, the cofounder of the Zero Proof Life, Christy; their son; and two shih-poos, Archie and Oscar. Their daughter is in college. You can learn more about Billy's writing, teaching, and coaching at BillyWynne.com.